A GUIDE TO

LOVE'S LABOUR'S LOST

The Shakespeare Handbooks

Guides available now:

- Antony and Cleopatra
- As You Like It
- The Comedy of Errors
- Coriolanus
- Cymbeline
- Hamlet
- Henry IV, Part 1
- Julius Caesar
- King Lear
- Love's Labour's Lost
- Macbeth
- Measure for Measure
- The Merchant of Venice
- The Merry Wives of Windsor
- A Midsummer Night's Dream
- Much Ado About Nothing
- Othello
- Richard II
- Richard III
- Romeo and Juliet
- The Tempest
- Twelfth Night
- The Winter's Tale

Further titles in preparation.

The Shakespeare Handbooks

A Guide to

Love's Labour's Lost

by Alistair McCallum

Upstart Crow Publications

First published in 2023 by
Upstart Crow Publications

Copyright © Alistair McCallum 2023

A CIP catalogue record for this book
is available from the British Library

ISBN 978 1 899747 23 8

Printed in Great Britain by Print2Demand Ltd,
1 Newlands Road, Westoning,
Bedfordshire MK45 5LD

www.shakespeare-handbooks.com

Setting the scene

Shakespeare probably wrote *Love's Labour's Lost* during the period 1594–6. He had just turned thirty, and was already a rising star in the world of London theatre.

Having left his home town of Stratford-upon-Avon in his early twenties, Shakespeare had started as a novice actor, but quickly turned to writing. His success soon attracted the envious attention of the established London author Robert Greene, who in 1592 scathingly described the provincial newcomer, the actor-turned-playwright who lacked a university education, as 'an upstart crow, beautified with our feathers'.

In 1594, Shakespeare took the significant step of becoming a member – and shareholder – of a newly-formed company of actors, the Lord Chamberlain's Men: they were soon to become London's most successful theatre company, and Shakespeare would go on to work with the same group for the rest of his career. *Love's Labour's Lost* was one of the first plays – possibly the first – that Shakespeare wrote for the new company. The play was immediately popular, both at the public theatres and at private performances for Queen Elizabeth's court.

Love's Labour's Lost is a bright, witty comedy that revels in the use – and abuse – of language. Shakespeare mocks the linguistic excesses and sophistication of courtly life in this play; at the same time, he clearly enjoys indulging himself in the characters' constant games of wordplay. In *Love's Labour's Lost*, there is more verse – in the form of rhyming couplets, songs, poems, even complete sonnets – than in any other Shakespeare play:

"We all have particular favorites, in literature as in life, and I take more unmixed pleasure from Love's Labour's Lost *than from any other Shakespearean play ... I entertain the illusion that Shakespeare may have enjoyed a particular and unique zest in composing it.* Love's Labour's Lost *is a festival of language, an exuberant fireworks display in which Shakespeare seems to seek the limits of his verbal resources, and discovers that there are none."*

Harold Bloom, *Shakespeare: The Invention of the Human*, 1998

A devotion to knowledge

Nestled in the Pyrenees between France and Spain lies the little Kingdom of Navarre, ruled over by King Ferdinand. Although his kingdom is small, Ferdinand has great ambitions: he is determined that Navarre will be known throughout the world, and for all time, as a byword for learning, art and philosophy.

With this in mind, the king has enlisted the help of three young courtiers to join him in forming a group of dedicated scholars who, setting aside all worldly pleasures, will devote their lives entirely to study for the next three years.

Two of the courtiers, full of enthusiasm and idealism, are eager to begin their noble undertaking. The third, although he has agreed in principle, has misgivings. He is troubled, in particular, by one condition that the king has imposed on the foursome: for the duration of their three-year pursuit of knowledge, female company is strictly forbidden.

Curtain up

Good intentions I, i

King Ferdinand is addressing three of his lords, Longaville, Dumaine and Berowne.

Achieving a glorious reputation, the king declares, should be the true aim of life; only those who do so will live on, in name, after their death. This is the purpose of his present plan for himself and his three companions:

King: Let fame, that all hunt after in their lives,
Live registered upon our brazen tombs,[1]
And then grace us in the disgrace of death;[2]
When, spite of cormorant devouring Time,[3]
Th'endeavour of this present breath may buy
That honour which shall bate his scythe's keen edge,
And make us heirs of all eternity.[4]

[1] *be inscribed on brass plaques on our graves*
[2] *make us honoured even when our bodies have been
disfigured by death*
[3] *in spite of Time, which devours everything like an
aggressive, ravenous bird*
[4] *the efforts that we make in our lifetimes may bring us
honour that will blunt the edge of Time's sharp scythe,
and keep our memory alive for ever*

Ferdinand's proposal is that he and his friends should spend three years completely isolated from worldly affairs, devoting themselves instead to study and scholarly contemplation. The king's ambition is not just for himself and his companions, however. His court, and indeed the whole country, will become renowned far and wide:

King: Navarre shall be the wonder of the world;
Our court shall be a little academe,[1]
Still and contemplative in living art.[2]

[1] *like the famed Academy of Plato in ancient Greece*
[2] *calmly and steadily studying life's essential knowledge*

The three courtiers have already agreed to dedicate themselves, along with the king, to a secluded life of learning for the next three years. The king now demands their written assurance that they will remain faithful to their promise. He has drawn up a document setting out the rules that will govern their lives during the long period of study, and he asks his friends to sign it.

Two of the lords consent enthusiastically. They are only too willing, they claim, to abstain from the pleasures of the world:

King:	Your oaths are passed, and now subscribe[1] your names,
	That his own hand may strike his honour down
	That violates the smallest branch herein[2] ...
Longaville:	I am resolved. 'Tis but a three years' fast.
	The mind shall banquet, though the body pine.[3]
	Fat paunches have lean pates[4] ...
Dumaine:	My loving lord, Dumaine is mortified.[5]
	The grosser manner of these world's delights
	He throws upon the gross world's baser slaves.[6]

[1] *sign*
[2] *so that any man who disobeys a single clause of this agreement will be shown, by his own hand, to be dishonourable*
[3] *starve*
[4] *a full, well-fed belly is a sign of a weak mind*
[5] *dead to worldly gratification*
[6] *I leave the cruder kinds of pleasure to inferior people who are addicted to such things*

Shakespeare seems to have been an avid reader as well as a keen observer of human nature. However, unlike most literary figures of his time, he did not go to university:

"The premise of the King's exercise is that there is no place for love in intellectual life. Shakespeare, who did not of course spend three years in the all-male environment of an Oxford or Cambridge college, clearly thought that this was nonsense ..."

Jonathan Bate, *Soul of the Age*, 2008

A reluctant recruit

The third lord, Berowne, is more hesitant. He has agreed to engage in a long period of study with the others, but suspects that the conditions imposed by the king will be too harsh.

Aware that the king has in mind a three-year period of complete abstinence and self-denial, Berowne looks dubiously at the document that his friends have signed. He is unwilling to agree to it, he declares, if its contents are as extreme as he fears:

Berowne: So much, dear liege,[1] I have already sworn,
That is, to live and study here three years.
But there are other strict observances:
As[2] not to see a woman in that term,
Which I hope well is not enrolled there;[3]
And one day in a week to touch no food,
And but[4] one meal on every day beside,
The which I hope is not enrolled there;
And then to sleep but three hours in the night ...
O, these are barren tasks, too hard to keep,
Not to see ladies, study, fast, not sleep.

[1] *sovereign, king*
[2] *such as*
[3] *listed, included in the document*
[4] *only, no more than*

The others retort that Berowne is well aware of the nature of the agreement, and has already given his word. Berowne shrugs off the accusation:

King: Your oath is passed to pass away from these.[1]
Berowne: Let me say no, my liege, an if you please.
I only swore to study with your Grace,
And stay here in your court for three years' space.
Longaville: You swore to that, Berowne, and to the rest.
Berowne: By yea and nay,[2] sir, then I swore in jest.

[1] *you have taken an oath to give up these pleasures*
[2] *I wasn't being serious; I swore and I didn't swear*

The pursuit of knowledge should be enlightening and enjoyable, argues Berowne; it is perverse to make it tedious and unrewarding. Learning can even be harmful if it is separated from the pleasures of life. Reading for hours on end, for example, is futile if it only results in poor eyesight. Berowne's language becomes more and more extravagant as he warms to his theme:

Berowne: Why, all delights are vain,[1] but that most vain
Which, with pain purchased, doth inherit pain:[2]
As[3] painfully to pore upon a book
To seek the light of truth, while truth the while
Doth falsely blind the eyesight of his look.[4]
Light seeking light doth light of light beguile[5] ...

[1] *pointless, unproductive*
[2] *the most pointless activity of all is one which is
unpleasant and only produces further suffering*
[3] *such as; for example*
[4] *the search for truth, meanwhile, treacherously
deprives the reader of his eyesight*
[5] *the eyes, in seeking truth, deprive themselves of
the power of sight (eyes were believed to produce
beams of light which enabled them to see)*

Learning can become arid and meaningless if it is cut off from the emotions and experiences of everyday life, insists Berowne. He gives the example of an astronomer who spends his nights cataloguing the stars in the sky:

Berowne: Small have continual plodders ever won,
Save base authority from others' books.[1]
These earthly godfathers of heaven's lights,
That give a name to every fixed star,[2]
Have no more profit of their shining nights
Than those that walk and wot not what they are.[3]

[1] *conscientious drudges have never learnt much other
than commonplace, second-hand knowledge*
[2] *astronomers who give names to all the stars*
[3] *do not appreciate the starry nights more than those
who simply walk under the open sky with no idea of
the stars' names*

The others dismiss Berowne's arguments; he appears to be rejecting the value of learning even though he is clearly a learned and articulate man himself. The king, unwilling to discuss the matter further, tells Berowne that he is free to change his mind and leave the little band of scholars.

However, Berowne now declares that, having made a promise, he will be as good as his word. Setting his reservations aside, he announces that he will sign the agreement, no matter how severe the conditions may be. The king is delighted:

Berowne:	… I'll keep what I have sworn,
	And bide the penance of each three years' day.[1]
	Give me the paper, let me read the same,
	And to the strictest decrees I'll write my name.
King:	How well this yielding[2] rescues thee from shame!

[1] *endure the harsh restrictions for every day of our three-year mission*
[2] *giving way to persuasion, changing your mind*

As Berowne peruses the agreement, he notices that, as he expected, it forbids any contact with women throughout the long period of study. He points out that the king himself is likely to break this rule in the near future, as the daughter of the King of France is due to visit Navarre soon on a diplomatic mission. King Ferdinand, taken aback, turns to his courtiers:

Berowne:	[*reads*] '… If any man be seen to talk with a woman within the term of three years, he shall endure such public shame as the rest of the court can possibly devise.'
	This article, my liege, yourself must break,
	For well you know here comes in embassy
	The French king's daughter with yourself to speak …
King:	What say you, lords? Why, this was quite forgot.

Berowne cannot resist teasing the king about his oversight. In his enthusiasm for scholarship and learning, he has failed to give any thought to his everyday duties. The king, exasperated, decides that the rule regarding female company can be set aside on this one occasion.

Berowne suspects that there will be many more such occasions over the next few years. As he puts his name to the agreement, he suggests, enigmatically, that despite his reluctance he will keep to the rules for longer than his companions:

King: We must of force[1] dispense with this decree.
         She must lie here on mere necessity.[2]
Berowne: Necessity will make us all forsworn[3]
         Three thousand times within this three years' space ...
         But I believe, although I seem so loath,
         I am the last that will keep his oath. [*signs*]

[1] *necessarily, inevitably*
[2] *it is absolutely necessary for the princess to lodge at court*
[3] *will make us all break our oaths*

The idea that female company was inimical to men's learning and spiritual development was widespread in Shakespeare's time. In 1571, the Fellows of Trinity College, Cambridge – whose aim was to educate future leaders of the newly-reformed Church of England – decreed that *"all young women shal be banished and putt out of the college"* and if any scholar *"under any pretext bring any young woman into the College to entertaine, maintaine, or employ them"* he would be fined and *"publickly corrected in the hall with the rodd."*

A minor offence

Berowne wonders what the four of them will do for entertainment, given the restrictions under which they have agreed to live. The king mentions a character who frequently keeps them amused without realising it, a pompous, boastful Spaniard with an erratic command of English. The name of the Spanish nobleman, a guest at the court of Navarre, is Don Adriano de Armado.

Another individual who may be a source of diversion is the clownish servant Costard; and just as his name is mentioned, Costard himself appears. He is evidently in trouble, as he is accompanied by the local constable, Anthony Dull. The constable produces a letter for the king from Don Armado, apparently concerning an offence committed by Costard. The situation is unclear, however, as both Dull and Costard are eccentric in their use of language:

Dull:	Which is the Duke's own person? [1]
Berowne:	[*indicates the king*] This, fellow. What wouldst? [2]
Dull:	I myself reprehend [3] his own person, for I am his Grace's farborough. [4] But I would see his own person in flesh and blood.
Berowne:	This is he.
Dull:	[*to the king*] Signior Arm… Arm…[5] commends you. There's villainy abroad.[6] This letter will tell you more.
Costard:	Sir, the contempts [7] thereof are as touching me.

[1] *which one of you is the king?*
[2] *what do you want?*
[3] *represent*
[4] *the king's constable*
[5] *Dull is unable to pronounce 'Armado'*
[6] *going on, taking place*
[7] *contents*

The king reads the letter aloud. Don Armado's prose is lengthy and convoluted, but it eventually becomes clear that, while taking a walk in the evening, he saw something that shocked him:

King:	[*reads*] '*Great deputy, the welkin's viceregent,[1] and sole dominator of Navarre … besieged with sable-coloured melancholy, I did commend the black*

oppressing humour to the most wholesome physic of thy health-giving air [2] ... The time When? About the sixth hour, when beasts most graze, birds best peck, and men sit down to that nourishment which is called supper. So much for the time when. Now for the ground Which – which, I mean, I walked upon. It is yclept [3] thy park. Then for the place Where – where, I mean, I did encounter that obscene and most preposterous event that draweth from my snow-white pen the ebon-coloured ink [4] ...'

[1] *the ruler appointed by Heaven*
[2] *feeling depressed, I decided to go outdoors for a walk*
[3] *called, known as*
[4] *that compels me to write*

It emerges that Armado saw Costard making advances towards the dairymaid Jaquenetta. Navarre has strict laws against such liaisons, the king points out: these laws are well known, and Costard must be aware of them. The young man tries to claim that he has not broken the letter of the law:

King:	… sirrah, what say you to this?
Costard:	Sir, I confess the wench. [1]
King:	Did you hear the proclamation?
Costard:	I do confess much of the hearing it, but little of the marking of it. [2]
King:	It was proclaimed a year's imprisonment to be taken with a wench.
Costard:	I was taken with none, sir, I was taken with a damsel.
King:	Well, it was proclaimed 'damsel'.
Costard:	This was no damsel neither, sir, she was a virgin.
King:	It is so varied too, [3] for it was proclaimed 'virgin'.
Costard:	If it were, I deny her virginity.

[1] *that I was with the young woman*
[2] *I did not take much notice of it*
[3] *the announcement allowed for that too*

Although *Love's Labour's Lost* was undoubtedly popular when first produced, the play fell out of favour for at least two hundred years following Shakespeare's death: some later critics did not even consider it to be the work of Shakespeare. The prominent 18th-century writer Samuel Johnson defended the play, despite his reservations:

"In this play, which all the editors have concurred to censure, and some have rejected as unworthy of our poet, it must be confessed that there are many passages mean, childish, and vulgar; and some which ought not to have been exhibited, as we are told they were, to a maiden queen. But there are scattered through the whole many sparks of genius ..."

Dr Johnson, *The Plays of William Shakespeare*, 1765

Costard's arguments fall on deaf ears. However, the king, amused by Armado's letter, dismisses the young man with an insignificant punishment, to be supervised by the offended Spaniard:

King:	Sir, I will pronounce your sentence: you shall fast a week with bran[1] and water.
Costard:	I had rather pray a month with mutton and porridge.
King:	And Don Armado shall be your keeper.

[1] *bread made from coarse, inferior grain*

Eager to start on his long interlude of scholarship and seclusion, the king sets off with his companions. Berowne remains sceptical:

King:	... go we, lords, to put in practice that Which each to other hath so strongly sworn. [*he leaves with Longaville and Dumaine*]
Berowne:	I'll lay my head to any goodman's hat,[1] These oaths and laws will prove an idle scorn.[2]

[1] *I'll bet my head against any common man's hat*
[2] *will become worthless objects of ridicule*

A lover's lament

Don Armado is talking to his young attendant Moth. The Spaniard tells the boy that he is in low spirits. He is in love, he complains: the emotion is not fitting for a valiant knight, he believes, and, to make things worse, the object of his love is a low-born woman. He wishes he could fight with his passion, defeat it and deliver it, like a hostage, to his enemy:

Armado: I will hereupon confess I am in love; and as it is base [1] for a soldier to love, so am I in love with a base wench. If drawing my sword against the humour of affection [2] would deliver me from the reprobate [3] thought of it, I would take Desire prisoner, and ransom him to any French courtier ...

[1] *ignoble, disreputable*
[2] *inclination to fall in love*
[3] *corrupt, sinful*

Armado asks the pageboy to suggest other illustrious warriors who, like him, have fallen in love. He is pleased with the boy's suggestions, revelling in a sense of fellow-feeling with the great heroes of the past:

Armado: Comfort me, boy: what great men have been in love?
Moth: Hercules, master.
Armado: Most sweet Hercules! More authority,[1] dear boy, name more; and, sweet my child, let them be men of good repute and carriage.[2]
Moth: Samson,[3] master, he was a man of good carriage, great carriage, for he carried the town gates on his back like a porter, and he was in love.
Armado: O well-knit Samson, strong-jointed Samson! I do excel thee in my rapier as much as thou didst me in carrying gates. I am in love too.

[1] *examples from history*
[2] *demeanour, behaviour*
[3] *biblical hero of enormous strength who heaved the city gates of Gaza onto his back and carried them away*

Armado wonders whether he should write a ballad about the pain of falling in love with a woman so far beneath his own status. He then reveals that the object of his affections is none other than Jaquenetta, the dairymaid pursued by Costard:

Armado: Is there not a ballad, boy, of 'The King and the
             Beggar'? … I will have that subject newly writ o'er,[1]
             that I may example my digression by some mighty
             precedent.[2] Boy, I do love that country girl that I took[3]
             in the park with the rational hind[4] Costard. She
             deserves well.[5]

   [1] *I will get someone to adapt the story*
   [2] *so that I can justify my moral lapse by showing that
       great men of the past have been in the same situation*
   [3] *discovered, caught*
   [4] *rustic creature, barely capable of reason*
   [5] *a better man*

At this point the constable Dull arrives with Costard and Jaquenetta in tow. He explains that Armado is to oversee Costard's punishment, while the girl will be confined to her workplace. Armado cannot hide his feelings for Jaquenetta:

Dull: Sir, the Duke's[1] pleasure is that you keep Costard
             safe;[2] and you must suffer him to take no delight nor
             no penance,[3] but 'a[4] must fast three days a week. For
             this damsel, I must keep her at the park; she is allowed
             for the dey-woman.[5] Fare you well.
Armado: [*aside*] I do betray myself with blushing.

   [1] *king's*
   [2] *secure, in detention*
   [3] *Dull means 'pleasure'*
   [4] *he*
   [5] *permitted to work as the dairymaid*

Armado makes a clumsy attempt to declare his love, but Jaquenetta is unimpressed. As she is led away by Dull, the Spaniard turns angrily to Costard, vowing to punish him severely. He orders Moth to take the young man away and lock him up.

Now alone, Armado reflects, in his usual elaborate style, on the power of love. He cannot suppress his passion for the lowly Jaquenetta:

Armado: I do affect[1] the very ground (which is base) where her shoe (which is baser) guided by her foot (which is basest) doth tread ... Love is a devil. There is no evil angel but Love.

[1] *love, adore*

He realises that, although he is invincible as a warrior, he cannot win in the fight against Cupid. There is only one answer, he decides. He must resort to poetry:

Armado: ... His disgrace is to be called boy,[1] but his glory is to subdue men. Adieu, valour; rust, rapier; be still, drum; for your manager[2] is in love. Yea, he loveth. Assist me, some extemporal god of rhyme,[3] for I am sure I shall turn sonnet.[4] Devise, wit; write, pen ...

[1] *we insult Cupid by referring to him as a boy*
[2] *your master, the man who normally makes use of these things*
[3] *god of spontaneous verse*
[4] *become a sonneteer*

The name 'Armado' is undoubtedly a satirical reference to the Spanish Armada of 1588; the failed attempt to invade England and depose Queen Elizabeth was still fresh in people's memories when *Love's Labour's Lost* was first performed. The character may be partly based on an eccentric, deluded individual who frequented Queen Elizabeth's court, claiming – among other things – to be emperor of the world:

"Armado is a caricature of a half-crazed Spaniard known as 'the fantastical Monarcho' who for many years hung about Elizabeth's court, and was under the delusion that he owned the ships arriving in the port of London."

Charles Boyce, *Shakespeare A to Z*, 1990

Romance in the air

A royal party has arrived at the king's park: the French princess has come, as planned, on a diplomatic mission on behalf of her father the king. Her retinue includes Lord Boyet and three ladies-in-waiting. Boyet urges the princess to remember the importance of her task, which concerns the fate of the French territory of Aquitaine, part of which is currently held by Navarre. She will need to use all her abundant charisma, Boyet tells her, but the princess is unimpressed by his flattery:

Boyet:	Be now as prodigal of all dear grace
	As Nature was in making graces dear
	When she did starve the general world beside
	And prodigally gave them all to you.[1]
Princess:	Good Lord Boyet, my beauty, though but mean,[2]
	Needs not the painted flourish[3] of your praise.
	Beauty is bought by judgement of the eye,
	Not uttered by base sale of chapmen's tongues.[4]

[1] *be as lavish with your precious charm as Nature was when she bestowed so many attractive qualities on you, making them unavailable to everyone else*
[2] *only moderate*
[3] *superficial adornment*
[4] *not a commodity offered for sale by merchants*

The first thing that needs to be done, the princess declares, is to establish whether they will be permitted to meet King Ferdinand. News of the king's intention to spend a long period in seclusion, away from female company, has already travelled beyond Navarre:

Princess:	Good Boyet,
	You are not ignorant all-telling fame
	Doth noise abroad[1] Navarre hath made a vow,
	Till painful study shall outwear three years,[2]
	No woman may approach his silent[3] court.

[1] *you are aware of the news spread around by rumour, which reaches everyone*
[2] *until he has completed three years of arduous study*
[3] *quiet, deep in contemplation*

Accordingly, the princess decides to send Boyet to greet the king and ask whether he is prepared to meet her and her entourage. When Boyet has gone, the princess and her three attendants – Maria, Katherine and Rosaline – discuss the gentlemen who have vowed, along with the king, to shut themselves away for so long.

Maria reports that she has met one of the men, named Longaville, at a wedding party. She praises him highly, and confirms that his reputation as a gallant, handsome courtier is well deserved. His only fault, she suggests, is that he can be a little inconsiderate at times. The princess is sceptical:

Maria:	The only soil[1] of his fair virtue's gloss,
	If virtue's gloss will stain with any soil,
	Is a sharp wit matched with too blunt a will,[2]
	Whose edge hath power to cut, whose will still wills
	It should none spare that come within his power.[3]
Princess:	Some merry mocking lord, belike:[4] is't so?
Maria:	They say so most that most his humours know.[5]
Princess:	Such short-lived wits do wither as they grow.[6]

[1] *blemish*
[2] *a keen sense of humour which he is too ready to use, regardless of the circumstances*
[3] *his wit can be cutting, and is merciless once it has chosen its victim*
[4] *no doubt*
[5] *that's the view of those who best know his character*
[6] *if his wit is so brilliant, it will soon fade; his appeal won't last*

... a sharp wit matched with too blunt a will ...

The word 'wit' is used more often in *Love's Labour's Lost* than in any other Shakespeare play.

Katherine now reveals that she has met Dumaine, another of the lords in question. He is rightly famed for his virtue and his elegance, she confirms:

Katherine: … he hath wit to make an ill shape good,[1]
And shape to win grace though he had no wit.[2]
I saw him at the Duke Alençon's once,
And much too little of that good I saw
Is my report to his great worthiness.[3]

[1] *the intelligence and sympathy to make bad things seem good*
[2] *an appearance that would attract people even if he were not intelligent*
[3] *my description falls short of the excellent qualities I observed in him*

Finally, Rosaline describes a pleasant hour spent in the company of Berowne, the third of the king's companions, renowned for his humour and quick-wittedness. The princess is astonished. Her three ladies-in-waiting all seem to be infatuated with the courtiers of Navarre:

Rosaline: … a merrier man,
Within the limit of becoming[1] mirth,
I never spent an hour's talk withal.[2]
    … aged ears play truant at his tales,[3]
And younger hearings are quite ravished,
So sweet and voluble[4] is his discourse.
Princess: God bless my ladies! Are they all in love,
That every one her own hath garnished
With such bedecking ornaments of praise?[5]

[1] *seemly, agreeable*
[2] *with*
[3] *older listeners abandon more serious matters in order to hear him speak*
[4] *fluent, delightful*
[5] *each of you adorns your chosen man with such extravagant words of praise*

An inauspicious meeting

At this point Boyet returns. The king is ready to greet them, he reports. They will not be able to lodge at the king's residence, however: along with his oath to avoid female company, the king has dismissed his palace staff in advance of his long period of seclusion. Instead, the French party will be accommodated in tents in the king's parkland:

Princess: Now, what admittance,[1] lord?
Boyet: ... thus much I have learnt:
He rather means to lodge you in the field,
Like one that comes here to besiege his court,[2]
Than seek a dispensation for his oath,[3]
To let you enter his unpeopled [4] house.

[1] *what does the king say about admitting us to court?*
[2] *in the grounds around his court, like an encircling army*
[3] *rather than find an excuse to break his oath*
[4] *unstaffed, devoid of servants*

The king now arrives, accompanied by his three courtiers. His greeting receives an unexpectedly blunt response. They are still outdoors, the princess points out, so it makes no sense for the king to welcome them to his court:

King: Fair princess, welcome to the court of Navarre.
Princess: 'Fair' I give you back again,[1] and 'welcome' I have
not yet. The roof of this court is too high to be yours,[2]
and welcome to the wide fields too base to be mine.[3]

[1] *I am not interested in your compliment*
[2] *you do not own the open air and the sky, so you cannot welcome me to them*
[3] *to welcome me to these open fields would be insulting*

The king, embarrassed, attempts to explain the oath that he and his companions have taken. The princess knows about the oath, she tells him impatiently; she considers it a foolish idea, as he will gain a reputation for ill-treatment of guests if he keeps it, or for breaking his word if he does not. She then apologises mockingly for her criticism. After all, he is now a renowned academic:

Princess: I hear your grace hath sworn out housekeeping:[1]
'Tis deadly sin to keep that oath, my lord,
And sin to break it.
But pardon me, I am too sudden bold;
To teach a teacher ill beseemeth me.[2]

[1] *has renounced hospitality*
[2] *is not my place, is inappropriate*

"The first exchange between the Princess and the King tells us much. 'Fair Princess, welcome to the court of Navarre', says he, mouthing the polite formula he thinks appropriate to the occasion and, no doubt, expecting a similar formula in return. He does not receive it ... It is already clear that, for her, words are not things to be twisted, turned, and given as much or as little weight as the speaker chooses. They should be the instruments of society, the servants of truth, and correspond with facts. Forced into facing his own discourtesy, Navarre tries to gloss it over, but only succeeds in making it worse ..."

G. R. Hibbard, Introduction to the Oxford
Shakespeare edition of *Love's Labour's Lost*, 1990

Difficult negotiations

Without further ado, the princess hands King Ferdinand a document outlining the matters that she wishes to discuss as representative of her father, the King of France. The sooner they can resolve these matters, she says brusquely, the sooner Ferdinand will be free of her:

Princess: Vouchsafe to read the purpose of my coming,
                And suddenly resolve me in my suit.[1]
                [she gives him a document]
King: Madam, I will, if suddenly I may.[2]
Princess: You will the sooner that I were away,
                For you'll prove perjured if you make me stay.[3]

[1] *grant me the favour of learning why I have come, and answering my request immediately*
[2] *if I can do so immediately, I will*
[3] *I expect you'll do it as quickly as possible in order to get rid of me, otherwise you'll be in danger of breaking your oath*

As the king withdraws to read the document, Berowne takes the opportunity to talk to Rosaline. He is sure he recognises her, but she offers him no encouragement:

Berowne: Did not I dance with you in Brabant once?
Rosaline: Did not I dance with you in Brabant once?
Berowne: I know you did.
Rosaline: How needless was it then
             To ask the question?
Berowne: You must not be so quick.[1]
Rosaline: 'Tis long of you that spur me[2] with such questions.
Berowne: Your wit's too hot,[3] it speeds too fast, 'twill tire.
Rosaline: Not till it leave the rider in the mire.[4]

[1] *sharp, impatient*
[2] *it's your fault for provoking me*
[3] *hasty, eager*
[4] *not until its victim is thrown into the mud*

King Ferdinand now returns. He immediately makes it clear that he is extremely unhappy with the contents of the princess's document. Ferdinand's father, the previous King of Navarre, had lent a large sum of money to the King of France to help finance his country's wars. As security for the loan, France had granted Navarre a small part of the territory of Aquitaine. France has since repaid part of the loan: King Ferdinand had assumed that the princess's visit was concerned with repayment of the remainder of the loan to Navarre, and the return of Aquitaine to France.

In the princess's document, however, the French king appears to deny that he owes any more money to Navarre. He does not even mention the portion of Aquitaine that is currently held by Navarre, a relatively insignificant piece of land that Ferdinand has no interest in keeping.

The princess and her attendant Lord Boyet insist that they have financial records proving that the French king is in the right. Those accounts are still on their way from France, and will be available shortly. In the meantime, the negotiations have reached a stalemate.

Despite the diplomatic quarrel, relations between the king and the princess appear to be thawing rapidly. Ferdinand assures her that he will be reasonable, and will accept any valid evidence produced by France. He promises that the princess's accommodation, although under canvas out in the fields, will be welcoming and agreeable, and they part on amicable terms:

King:	You may not come, fair Princess, within my gates,
	But here without[1] you shall be so received
	As[2] you shall deem yourself lodged in my heart,
	Though so denied fair harbour in my house.
	Your own good thoughts excuse me, and farewell.
	Tomorrow shall we visit you again.
Princess:	Sweet health and fair desires consort[3] your grace.

[1] *out here in my parkland*
[2] *so well treated that*
[3] *be with, attend*

As Ferdinand and his courtiers leave, Berowne briefly remains behind and again tries to ingratiate himself with Rosaline, without success:

Berowne: Lady, I will commend you to my own heart.
Rosaline: Pray you, do my commendations;[1] I would be glad to see it.[2]
Berowne: I would you heard it groan.[3]
Rosaline: Is the fool sick?
Berowne: Sick at the heart.
Rosaline: Alack, let it blood.[4]
Berowne: Would that do it good?
Rosaline: My physic[5] says ay.
Berowne: Will you prick't with your eye?
Rosaline: *Non point,*[6] with my knife.

[1] *please give my respects to your heart*
[2] *to see your heart out of your body*
[3] *I wish you could hear how my heart groans*
[4] *remove some of its blood*
[5] *medical knowledge*
[6] *not at all*

Making enquiries

The princess and her attendants are now alone. However, the three lords surreptitiously return, one by one, and each asks Boyet the name of the lady who has caught his eye. Dumaine arrives first: he learns that the woman in question is named Katherine. Next, Longaville comes to enquire about the woman he admires. Before revealing Maria's identity, Boyet teases him:

Longaville: I beseech you, a word. What[1] is she in the white?
Boyet: A woman sometimes, an[2] you saw her in the light.
Longaville: Perchance light in the light.[3] I desire her name.
Boyet: She hath but one for herself; to desire that were a shame.
Longaville: Pray you, sir, whose daughter?
Boyet: Her mother's, I have heard.

[1] *who*
[2] *if*
[3] *perhaps she will prove fickle when her true character emerges*

Berowne is the next to return. He is pleased with Boyet's answers:

Berowne: What's her name in the cap?
Boyet: Rosaline, by good hap.[1]
Berowne: Is she wedded or no?
Boyet: To her will, sir, or so.[2]

[1] *fortune*
[2] *you could say that she is married to her own*
   stubbornness

The French party is now in high spirits, amused by the spectacle of the courtiers creeping back, despite their vows, in pursuit of the three ladies-in-waiting. However, Boyet is confident that it is not just the courtiers who have fallen in love:

Boyet: If my observation, which very seldom lies
            By the heart's still rhetoric disclosed with eyes,[1]
            Deceive me not now, Navarre[2] is infected.

[1] *which is rarely mistaken in reading the silent, hidden*
   feelings revealed in a person's eyes
[2] *the king*

The princess claims not to know what he means, but Boyet persists; the king's feelings were there in his eyes, for all to see. Boyet indulges in a spell of poetic hyperbole, but his message is clear. King Ferdinand has fallen in love with the princess:

Boyet: Methought all his senses were locked in his eye,
            As jewels in crystal for some prince to buy,[1]
            Who, tendering their own worth from where they
               were glassed,
            Did point you to buy them along as you passed.[2]

[1] *like jewels displayed in a crystal case for the attention*
   of a royal buyer
[2] *which offered themselves from their glass casket,*
   appealing to you to buy them as you passed by

Boyet is talking nonsense, the princess declares briskly; besides, it is time to retire to their tent. The courtier claims that he is only reporting what he has seen:

Princess: Come, to our pavilion. Boyet is disposed.[1]

Boyet: But to speak that in words which his eye hath disclosed.[2]

[1] *inclined to be merry; mocking me*
[2] *I'm only inclined to put into words what was revealed in the king's eyes*

"Pastoral seems to be the perfect word for the mood of Love's Labour's Lost. *We are sequestered in a world where, although we meet people in various professions, no one is working. The constable seems to be taken up with no formal obligations, the King has no wars or plagues with which to contend – this is a playful world of the idle, the elite. We witness their diversions: intellectual pursuits, a hunting escapade, courtship games ... Nothing is to be taken too seriously. There is no sickness, no grief, no death – not here – not yet."*

Director Susan Baer Beck on her 1994 production of *Love's Labour's Lost* for the Nebraska Shakespeare Festival

Costard is set free

Don Armado, meanwhile, is still suffering the pangs of
unrequited love. He has written a passionate letter to his beloved
Jaquenetta, and decides to ask Costard to deliver it. He gives
his servant Moth the key for the room in which Costard is
currently imprisoned.

Before the boy leaves, he gives his master some advice on the
best way, according to the latest fashions, to win Jaquenetta's
heart. She should be wooed with dancing and singing, he
explains, together with a forlorn, dishevelled appearance:

Moth: ... jig off a tune at the tongue's end,[1] canary to it[2] with
your feet, humour it[3] with turning up your eyelids, sigh
a note and sing a note, sometime through the throat as
if you swallowed love with singing love, sometime
through the nose as if you snuffed up love by smelling
love, with your hat penthouse-like o'er the shop of your
eyes[4] ...

[1] *sing a tune in the style of a lively jig*
[2] *dance the canary (a lively Spanish dance) while
    you're singing*
[3] *adapt yourself to the song, show your emotions*
[4] *pulled down over your eyes, like the awning
    protecting a shop's merchandise*

Moth hurries away and returns with Costard, who is at first baffled
by the Spaniard's lofty language:

Armado: Sirrah Costard, I will enfranchise thee.
Costard: O, marry me to one Frances![1]
Armado: ... By my sweet soul, I mean setting thee at liberty,
enfreedoming thy person. Thou wert immured,[2]
restrained, captivated, bound.

[1] *'Frances' was a common term for a prostitute*
[2] *walled up, imprisoned*

In return for a simple task, Armado promises to set him free. He even gives Costard a small reward in advance:

Armado: I give thee thy liberty, set thee from durance,[1] and in lieu thereof[2] impose on thee nothing but this: [*hands him a letter*] bear this significant[3] to the country maid Jaquenetta. [*hands him a coin*] There is remuneration ...

[1] *release you from confinement*
[2] *in exchange*
[3] *message, letter*

When Armado and his pageboy have left, Costard contemplates the coin he has just been given. He is delighted both with his reward and with the new word he has just learnt, 'remuneration', assuming it to be the name of the coin. He will use the word in future, he decides, whenever the subject of money crops up.

Another love-letter

Berowne now appears on the scene. He has been looking for Costard; he too has a task for the young man. However, before Berowne can explain the nature of the errand, Costard is keen to find out more about his coin. Even though he knows it to be worth three-quarters of a penny, he is curious as to what it might buy. Berowne states the obvious, but his answer seems to satisfy Costard:

Berowne: My good knave Costard, exceedingly well met.
Costard: Pray you, sir, how much carnation[1] ribbon may a man buy for a remuneration?
Berowne: What is a remuneration?
Costard: Marry, sir, halfpenny-farthing.[2]
Berowne: Why then, three-farthing worth of silk.
Costard: I thank your worship. God be wi'you.

[1] *pink, flesh-coloured*
[2] *three farthings; three quarters of a penny*

Berowne's initial attempts to hold Costard's attention are unsuccessful:

Berowne:	As thou wilt win my favour, good my knave,
	Do one thing for me that I shall entreat.
Costard:	When would you have it done, sir?
Berowne:	This afternoon.
Costard:	Well, I will do it, sir. Fare you well.
Berowne:	Thou knowest not what it is.
Costard:	I shall know, sir, when I have done it.
Berowne:	Why, villain, thou must know first.

Eventually Berowne manages to make himself understood. He has an important letter, he tells Costard, and it is essential that it is delivered to the right person this afternoon. He too gives the young man a reward, a coin of much greater value than Armado's. Costard is overjoyed:

Berowne:	The Princess comes to hunt here in the park,
	And in her train there is a gentle lady;
	When tongues speak sweetly, then they name her name,
	And Rosaline they call her. Ask for her,
	And to her white hand see thou do commend
	This sealed-up counsel.[1] [*hands him a letter*] There's
	thy guerdon:[2] [*hands him a coin*] go.
Costard:	Gardon, O sweet gardon! Better than remuneration ...
	I will do it, sir, in print.[3] Gardon! Remuneration!

[1] *private message*
[2] *reward, payment*
[3] *I will follow your instructions precisely, down to the last detail*

Costard hurries away to deliver the letter. Berowne, now alone, reflects on his own transformation. He has always been cynical about love and its supposed effects, and has kept his own affections firmly under control:

Berowne:	... I, forsooth, in love! I that have been love's whip,[1]
	A very beadle to a humorous sigh,[2]
	A critic, nay, a night-watch constable,

A domineering pedant o'er the boy [3] ...

[1] *harsh enemy*
[2] *strictly guarding against any sign that I might be falling in love, such as a moody sigh (beadles were local officials responsible for punishing minor offenders, usually by whipping)*
[3] *a stern schoolmaster, keeping an eye on young Cupid*

Berowne realises that Cupid, though young, small, blindfolded and unpredictable, has captivated him. As a result, he finds himself attracted to a woman who will bring nothing but trouble:

Berowne: O my little heart!
And I to be a corporal of his field [1]
And wear his colours like a tumbler's hoop! [2]
What? I love, I sue, [3] I seek a wife?
A woman that is like a German clock,
Still a-repairing, ever out of frame
And never going aright [4] ...

[1] *I have become a foot-soldier in Cupid's army*
[2] *wear his insignia, like an acrobat's hoop adorned with ribbons*
[3] *pursue, court*
[4] *always needing attention, always out of order, never behaving properly (German clocks of the time were often highly decorative, but notoriously unreliable)*

In 1598, a few years after its first performances, *Love's Labour's Lost* was published in the form of a paperback booklet known as a 'quarto'. Several other plays had been published before, but this was the first quarto to include the author's name on the cover, which read:

"A pleasant conceited comedie called Loves Labors Lost. As it was presented before her Highnes this last Christmas. Newly corrected and augmented by W. Shakespere."

By this time, the name of the 34-year-old Shakespeare had clearly become established as a unique selling point.

Pursuing Rosaline will mean violating the oath that he has sworn, Berowne realises; yet this, and the mental turmoil he is going through, is all for the sake of a woman who, by rights, he should not even find attractive:

Berowne: Nay, to be perjured,[1] which is worst of all;
And among three [2] to love the worst of all;
A whitely wanton [3] with a velvet brow,
With two pitch-balls stuck in her face for eyes.[4]

[1] *to break my promise*
[2] *the three ladies-in-waiting*
[3] *a pale, headstrong woman*
[4] *with dark eyes, like lumps of tar*

He is being punished by Cupid, Berowne decides, and has no choice but to surrender and follow his heart. He will become exactly the kind of man who, in the past, he would have scorned:

Berowne: … And I to sigh for her, to watch [1] for her,
To pray for her! Go to! [2] It is a plague
That Cupid will impose for my neglect
Of his almighty dreadful little might.[3]
Well, I will love, write, sigh, pray, sue and groan.
Some men must love my lady, and some Joan.[4]

[1] *stay awake at night, lose sleep*
[2] *damn it*
[3] *his power that, even though he is just a child, is immense*
[4] *some men are drawn to a noble woman, and some to a lowly woman; love cannot choose*

An unwilling hunter

The French princess and her attendants are out in the park, hunting for deer. A forester, familiar with the local countryside, is accompanying the party. The princess asks him where she should position herself for a shot at the deer. She teases him over his answer, suggesting that he is commenting on her attractiveness:

Princess:	... Forester, my friend, where is the bush
	That we must stand and play the murderer[1] in?
Forester:	Hereby, upon the edge of yonder coppice,[2]
	A stand where you may make the fairest shoot.[3]
Princess:	I thank my beauty, I am fair that shoot,
	And thereupon thou speak'st 'the fairest shoot'.[4]

[1] *play the part of a murderer; kill a deer*
[2] *dense patch of trees and bushes*
[3] *concealed position from which you can get the best shot*
[4] *you're using the word 'fairest' to tell me how beautiful I am*

The forester hastily denies that he meant to compliment her. The princess teases him again, pretending to be offended, and the man becomes embarrassed:

Forester:	Pardon me, madam, for I meant not so.
Princess:	What, what? First praise me, and again[1] say no?
	O short-lived pride! Not fair? Alack for woe![2]
Forester:	Yes, madam, fair.[3]
Princess:	Nay, never paint me now.
	Where fair is not, praise cannot mend the brow.[4]
	Here, good my glass,[5] take this for telling true ...
	[*she gives him money*]

[1] *then, next*
[2] *so you're saying I'm not beautiful after all? That's devastating!*
[3] *but you are beautiful*
[4] *it's too late to flatter me now; compliments cannot create beauty where it does not exist*
[5] *mirror; my honest judge*

The princess now asks for her bow although, as a woman who considers herself merciful, she finds hunting distasteful. If she succeeds in killing a deer, she muses, her pleasure will come from receiving praise for her skill, not from the death of an innocent creature:

Princess: ... out of question so it is sometimes,
Glory grows guilty of detested crimes,[1]
When for fame's sake, for praise, an outward part,
We bend to that the working of the heart;[2]
As[3] I for praise alone now seek to spill
The poor deer's blood, that my heart means no ill.[4]

[1] *it is undoubtedly true that the pursuit of honour can drive people to commit dreadful acts*
[2] *when, for the sake of our reputation, and the superficial reward of people's admiration, we commit ourselves to unworthy aims*
[3] *in the same way*
[4] *means me no harm*

Hunting, which features both literally and metaphorically in *Love's Labour's Lost*, was a popular activity in Shakespeare's time. As Queen Elizabeth travelled around the country, deer hunts were often arranged for her; to ensure they were successful, the deer would be herded into a small area before the queen was handed a crossbow.

Like the French princess in this scene, Shakespeare's characters often express a degree of sympathy for hunted animals. This would have been very much a minority point of view, however, and certainly not one shared by the queen herself:

"A connection to the Elizabethan court seems likely in the deer-hunting scene, where the Princess and her ladies 'shoot' as Elizabeth herself did on more than one occasion ... there is no doubt that this scene reproduces a typical event for Elizabeth, who was frequently identified with Diana, the virgin huntress."

William C. Carroll, Introduction to the New Cambridge Shakespeare edition of *Love's Labour's Lost*, 2009

Boyet interjects, suggesting that the same might apply to domineering women who try to control their husbands; perhaps they are only interested in gaining a reputation. That is different, counters the princess: such women genuinely deserve any praise they receive, as they are acting in a worthy cause:

Boyet: Do not curst wives hold that self-sovereignty
              Only for praise' sake[1] when they strive to be
              Lords o'er their lords?[2]
Princess: Only for praise – and praise we may afford
              To any lady that subdues a lord.[3]

          [1] *don't overbearing wives behave in such an unruly
              way just to attract the approval of their peers*
          [2] *to dominate their husbands*
          [3] *yes, but we are right to praise any woman who gets
              the better of her husband*

The group's deliberations are interrupted by the arrival of a country bumpkin. It is Costard, and he is carrying a letter. The princess responds flippantly to the young man's enquiries:

Costard: Pray you, which is the head lady?
Princess: Thou shalt know her, fellow, by the rest that have
              no heads.
Costard: Which is the greatest lady, the highest?
Princess: The thickest[1] and the tallest.

          [1] *fattest*

Costard, however, takes the princess's words at face value, and unwittingly offends her with his bluntness:

Costard: The thickest and the tallest. It is so, truth is truth.
              An your waist, mistress, were as slender as my wit,
              One o'these maids' girdles for your waist should be fit.[1]
              Are not you the chief woman? You are the thickest here.
Princess: What's your will,[2] sir? What's you will?

          [1] *if your waist were as small as my intelligence, one
              of your maidservants' belts would easily fit you*
          [2] *what do you want?*

A misdirected message

Costard announces that he has a letter from the courtier Berowne to the lady-in-waiting Rosaline. The news causes great excitement among the French party, and the princess urges Boyet to open it and read it aloud. It immediately becomes obvious that Costard has delivered the wrong letter; this one is from Don Armado to the dairymaid Jaquenetta. Boyet reads it nevertheless. The language is effusive and overblown:

Boyet: [reads] 'By heaven, that thou art fair is most infallible; [1] true that thou art beauteous; truth itself that thou art lovely. More fairer than fair, beautiful than beauteous, truer than truth itself, have commiseration on thy heroic vassal.' [2]

[1] certain
[2] have pity on your heroic servant

The writer then launches into a tortuous, pedantic comparison with an old tale of a king who falls in love with a beggar-maid:

Boyet: [reads] 'Who came? The King. Why did he come? To see. Why did he see? To overcome. To whom came he? To the beggar. What saw he? The beggar. Who overcame he? The beggar. The conclusion is victory. On whose side? The King's. The captive is enriched. On whose side? The beggar's.'

In case the comparison is lost on the reader, the writer spells it out before declaring his undying love and signing his name:

Boyet: [reads] 'The catastrophe is a nuptial. [1] On whose side? The King's? No, on both in one, or one in both. I am the King, for so stands the comparison, thou the beggar, for so witnesseth thy lowliness [2] ... I profane my lips on thy foot, my eyes on thy picture and my heart on thy every part. Thine in the dearest design of industry, [3] Don Adriano de Armado.'

[1] the story ends with a marriage
[2] your lowly status suits the role
[3] with the most loving intentions

The listeners are delighted by the ludicrous contents of the letter. Even though it was sent in error, the princess offers it to Rosaline as a keepsake. No doubt Rosaline herself will receive something similar in the future, suggests the princess as she sets off with her fellow hunters:

Princess:	Thou, fellow, a word.
	Who gave thee this letter?
Costard:	I told you – my lord.
Princess:	To whom shouldst thou give it?
Costard:	From my lord to my lady.
Princess:	From which lord to which lady?
Costard:	From my lord Berowne, a good master of mine,
	To a lady of France that he called Rosaline.
Princess:	Thou hast mistaken his letter. Come, lords, away.
	[*gives Rosaline the letter*] Here, sweet, put up [1] this;
	'twill be thine [2] another day.

[1] *put away, keep*
[2] *your turn to receive a similar letter*

Boyet teases Rosaline about her secret admirer. He predicts that her future husband will grow horns – the mark of a man with an adulterous wife – within a year:

Boyet:	Who is the shooter? [1] Who is the shooter?
Rosaline:	Shall I teach you to know?
Boyet:	Ay, my continent of beauty.
Rosaline:	Why, she that bears the bow. [2]
	Finely put off! [3]
Boyet:	My lady goes to kill horns, but if thou marry,
	Hang me by the neck if horns that year miscarry. [4]

[1] *the suitor aiming to win your heart*
[2] *the princess, as she is the one carrying a bow*
[3] *evaded*
[4] *the princess has gone to kill horned beasts, but if you marry, there will be no shortage of horns (as you will prove unfaithful to your husband)*

If they are talking of unfaithful wives, replies Rosaline, Boyet needs to be careful:

Rosaline:	Well, then, I am the shooter.[1]
Boyet:	And who is your deer?
Rosaline:	If we choose by the horns, yourself come not near.[2] Finely put on[3] indeed!
Maria:	You still wrangle with her, Boyet, and she strikes at the brow.[4]
Boyet:	But she herself is hit lower. Have I hit her now?[5]

[1] *I'm the one carrying the bow*
[2] *if my victim is going to be the one with the biggest horns, you'd better keep out of the way*
[3] *well aimed; I've hit the target*
[4] *you keep arguing with her, and she has taken aim at your head*
[5] *but she has been stricken in the heart; am I right?*

Love's Labour's Lost is unusual among Shakespeare's plays in that it contains a large number of references to events, ideas, jokes and songs that were current in his own time. After its initial burst of popularity, the play quickly became unfashionable, and was largely neglected until the 20th century.

Modern directors often cut portions of the text and set the play in a different era in order to make it more meaningful and accessible. In one production, for example, the action took place in a wealthy, secluded estate on the East Coast of America on the eve of the First World War:

"I did not choose an Elizabethan setting, because I wanted to avoid drawing attention to the very objections that kept this play neglected for over 200 years – namely, its up-to-the-minute, contemporary 1590s jokes. Today, 400 years later, each punchline requires a page of footnotes."

Director Gavin Cameron-Webb on his 2008 production of *Love's Labour's Lost* for the Colorado Shakespeare Festival

---

Superior intellects

IV, ii

Some citizens of Navarre have been observing the royal hunt. The princess has succeeded in killing a deer, and the men are discussing the nature of the dead beast. There is a difference of opinion. One of the men, a pedantic schoolmaster named Holofernes, claims that the deer was a fully-grown, mature animal:

Holofernes: The deer was, as you know, *sanguis*, in blood,[1] ripe as the pomewater,[2] who now hangeth like a jewel in the ear of *caelum*, the sky, the welkin, the heaven, and anon falleth like a crab on the face of *terra*, the soil, the land, the earth.[3]

[1] *in prime condition*
[2] *a large, juicy apple*
[3] *the deer was at one moment in mid-air, like a jewel hanging in the sky, and the next moment fell to the ground like a crab-apple*

The schoolmaster's companion, a humble clergyman named Nathaniel, respectfully disagrees, despite his friend's grandiose language and his liberal use of Latin. Constable Dull is with them, and he, too, believes it was just a young deer:

Nathaniel: Truly, Master Holofernes, the epithets are sweetly varied, like a scholar at the least.[1] But, sir, I assure ye it was a buck of the first head.[2]
Holofernes: Sir Nathaniel, *haud credo*.[3]
Dull: 'Twas not an old grey doe, 'twas a pricket.[4]

[1] *your description is wonderfully rich, and scholarly to say the least*
[2] *a deer whose antlers have just started to develop*
[3] *(Latin) I don't believe you*
[4] *a two-year-old deer*

39

Holofernes is disdainful of the constable's lack of learning. Nathaniel urges him to be grateful for such ignorance, as it serves to emphasise their own erudition and refinement:

Holofernes: O thou monster Ignorance, how deformed dost thou look!

Nathaniel: Sir, he hath never fed of the dainties[1] that are bred in a book.

He hath not eat paper, as it were; he hath not drunk ink.

His intellect is not replenished; he is only an animal, only sensible in the duller parts.[2]

And such barren plants are set before us that[3] we thankful should be –

Which we of taste and feeling are – for those parts that do fructify in us more than he.[4]

[1] *delicacies, delights*
[2] *only capable of experiencing more basic feelings*
[3] *so that*
[4] *for those qualities that have come to fruition in us rather than in him*

As a mark of his own brilliance, Holofernes offers to recite an impromptu poem in memory of the deer:

Holofernes: Sir Nathaniel, will you hear an extemporal[1] epitaph on the death of the deer?

Nathaniel: … Perge,[2] good Master Holofernes, *perge*, so it shall please you to abrogate scurrility.[3]

Holofernes: I will something affect the letter, for it argues facility.[4]

[1] *spontaneous, off-the-cuff*
[2] *(Latin) proceed*
[3] *as long as you agree to avoid lewdness*
[4] *I will use a certain amount of alliteration, as it demonstrates expertise with language*

On hearing the schoolmaster's extravagant, convoluted verse, Nathaniel is full of admiration. Dull is not impressed by the clergyman's obsequious attitude:

Holofernes: 'The preyful[1] Princess pierced and pricked a pretty pleasing pricket;[2]
Some say a sore,[3] but not a sore till now made sore with shooting ...'
Nathaniel: A rare talent!
Dull: If talent be a claw, look how he claws him with a talent.[4]

[1] *intent on killing her prey, ruthless*
[2] *wounded a lovely young deer with her bow and arrow*
[3] *some claim it was a four-year-old deer*
[4] *Nathaniel is scratching his companion's back, flattering him ('talent' was an alternative spelling of 'talon')*

"Shakespeare and his contemporaries attended 'grammar schools' in which they received a basic education in English and Latin grammar, along with mathematics, music, and astronomy. Many of the impressive-sounding Latin (and other) references in Love's Labors Lost *are actually the tritest of the exercises these young boys had to memorize and repeat out loud on a daily basis. Elizabethan audiences of every class would easily have gotten the jokes in the misquoting and mangling of many of the most basic passages from their education. The schoolmaster (or pedant), together with the local pastor (or curate) were often the most learned men in small country towns, although how learned they actually were could vary widely."*

Joanne Zipay, Programme notes for the Judith Shakespeare Company's production of *Love's Labour's Lost*, 2003

A harsh critic

The men's discussion is interrupted by the entrance of the dairymaid Jaquenetta. She is accompanied by Costard, who, she explains, has just handed her a letter from Don Armado. Unable to read herself, she has come to ask the clergyman Nathaniel to read it for her.

It immediately becomes clear that the letter consists of a sonnet, an elaborate poetic address to the writer's beloved. The author is torn between his love on the one hand and his oath to abstain from female company on the other:

Nathaniel: [*reads*] '*If love make me forsworn, how shall I swear to love?* [1]
Ah, never faith could hold, if not to beauty vowed! [2]
Though to myself forsworn, to thee I'll faithful prove;
Those thoughts to me were oaks, to thee like osiers bowed [3] ... '

[1] *if loving you means that I break my word, how can I give my word that I love you?*
[2] *the only vow I can keep is to beauty such as yours*
[3] *my earlier promises, which I had thought as strong as oaks, bend like willow branches under your influence*

The writer wants to gaze into his sweetheart's eyes rather than read books; and the only knowledge that now interests him is to become better acquainted with her. He ends by pleading with his beloved not to be angry with him for approaching her in this way. His future happiness, he claims, lies in her hands:

Nathaniel: [*reads*] '*Thy eye Jove's lightning bears, thy voice his dreadful* [1] *thunder,*
Which, not to anger bent, [2] *is music and sweet fire.*
Celestial as thou art, O, pardon love this wrong,
That sings heaven's praise [3] *with such an earthly tongue.*'

[1] *fearsome, awe-inspiring*
[2] *when not inclined to anger*
[3] *forgive my love its sin in daring to address heaven*

Holofernes takes hold of the letter irritably. Nathaniel has not read it correctly, he complains. Besides, it is a very poor effort, written by someone who, unlike himself, clearly has no understanding of poetry:

Holofernes: Let me supervise the canzonet.[1] [*takes the letter*] Here are only numbers ratified,[2] but for the elegancy, facility, and golden cadence of poesy, *caret*.[3]

> [1] *examine the little poem*
> [2] *the only good thing about it is that it scans; it is metrically correct*
> [3] *(Latin) it is lacking; it is a failure*

When Holofernes reads the remainder of the contents, it becomes clear that Costard has, again, delivered the wrong letter. In his usual wordy and pedantic manner, Holofernes explains that it is not from Armado but from one of the king's courtiers, and the intended recipient is not Jaquenetta:

Holofernes: I will overglance the superscript.[1] *'To the snow-white hand of the most beauteous Lady Rosaline ... Your Ladyship's in all desired employment,[2] Berowne.'*
... this Berowne is one of the votaries[3] with the King, and here he hath framed a letter to a sequent of the stranger Queen's,[4] which accidentally, or by way of progression,[5] hath miscarried.[6]

> [1] *cast an eye over the introduction*
> [2] *who will do whatever you ask*
> [3] *fellow oath-takers*
> [4] *he has written this letter to one of the French princess's attendants*
> [5] *as a consequence of the route it has taken*
> [6] *has failed to reach its destination*

With that, Holofernes sends Jaquenetta off to deliver the letter to the king. Turning to Nathaniel, he raises the subject of the poem they have just read. The clergyman suggests that the handwriting, at least, was admirable.

Holofernes mentions that he will be having lunch with the father of one of his pupils. If Nathaniel cares to join them, he promises, he will explain to his audience, in detail, exactly what is wrong with Berowne's sonnet. Constable Dull, who has been silent throughout their lengthy exchanges, is invited too.

Another poet   IV, iii

Berowne, still tormented by his love for Rosaline, is wandering, alone, holding a sheet of paper; he has been writing more poetry. While the king and the others are out hunting, he reflects, he is being relentlessly pursued by his own emotions. He tries to suppress his feelings for Rosaline, but without success:

Berowne: I will not love; if I do, hang me! I'faith, I will not.
          O, but her eye! [1] ... By heaven, I do love, and it hath
          taught me to rhyme, and to be melancholy ...

          [1] *how beautiful her eyes are!*

He glances at the sad lines he has written, and wonders how Rosaline reacted to the sonnet he has already sent. It occurs to him that his companions may be suffering in the same way. It would not worry him in the slightest if they were:

Berowne: ... here is part of my rhyme, and here my melancholy.
          Well, she hath one o'my sonnets already. The clown [1]
          bore it, the fool [2] sent it, and the lady hath it ... By the
          world, I would not care a pin if the other three were in. [3]

          [1] *Costard*
          [2] *I, Berowne*
          [3] *in the same predicament, in love*

At this moment the king passes by, and Berowne hastily takes cover. The king who, like Berowne, is carrying a sheet of paper, lets out a dramatic sigh. Berowne is delighted. The king is clearly in love, just like him:

King: Ay me!
Berowne: [*aside*] Shot, by heaven! Proceed, sweet Cupid, thou
          hast thumped him with thy birdbolt under the left pap. [1]

          [1] *you have hit him in the heart with your arrow*

The king, unaware of the eavesdropper, reads his poem aloud. In it, he laments that his tears are unceasing, and through them all he can see is his beloved's face. If she could see him, she would realise the power she has over him:

King: [reads] '... *Thou shin'st in every tear that I do weep,*
No drop but [1] *as a coach doth carry thee:*
So ridest thou triumphing in my woe. [2]
Do but behold the tears that swell in me,
And they thy glory through my grief will show.' [3]

[1] *every single teardrop*
[2] *when I cry, you ride triumphant in my tears*
[3] *in my grief, my tears will show your splendour*

At the end of the poem, the identity of his beloved is revealed. It is the French princess:

King: [reads] '*O Queen of queens, how far dost thou excel,*
No thought can think, nor tongue of mortal tell.'

"Shakespearian comedy is acutely aware that characters in love are simultaneously at their most 'real' and 'unreal', most true and most feigning ... The most 'natural' human activity is thus a question of high artifice, as is perhaps most obvious when Shakespearian characters write their love to each other, deploying stilted literary formulae to articulate that which supposedly beggars all description. Love's Labour's Lost *is much preoccupied with such ironic discrepancies between high-falutin poetic discourse and the plain impulses of sexual attraction.*"

Terry Eagleton, *William Shakespeare*, 1986

Guilty lovers

While the king is wondering how to make his feelings known to the princess, another figure approaches: it is Longaville. The king, startled, quickly hides from the courtier.

Longaville, too, is apparently in love. He is sighing in anguish, tortured both by his adoration of the French lady-in-waiting Maria and by the thought of breaking his vow. Berowne and the king, from their separate hiding-places, comment on their friend's emotional state. They are both relieved to see that they are not alone in failing to live up to their ideals:

Longaville: Ay me, I am forsworn![1]
King: ... [*aside*] In love, I hope. Sweet fellowship in shame.
Berowne: [*aside*] One drunkard loves another of the name.
Longaville: Am I the first that have been perjured so?
Berowne: [*aside*] I could put thee in comfort: not by two[2] that I know.

[1] *I have broken my promise*
[2] *by at least two people*

Longaville has attempted to put his feelings into verse, and is carrying a batch of papers with him. He looks disapprovingly at one poem, and decides to tear it up and try again:

Longaville: I fear these stubborn lines lack power to move.[1]
              [*reads*] *'O sweet Maria, empress of my love'* –
              These numbers[2] will I tear, and write in prose.

[1] *these awkward lines will not make her fall in love*
[2] *verses*

Another sonnet, he decides, is fit to send to his beloved. It justifies the fact that he is breaking his vow, as his worship of the divine Maria surpasses any worldly declarations he may have made:

Longaville: [*reads*] '*A woman I forswore, but I will prove,*
Thou being a goddess, I forswore not thee.[1]
My vow was earthly, thou a heavenly love;
Thy grace being gained cures all disgrace in me.'[2]

> [1] *I swore to avoid women, but I can prove that my vow did not apply to you, as your are a goddess*
> [2] *if I win your favour, my honour will remain unblemished*

It would be folly, he argues, to sacrifice his place in heaven for the sake of a few misguided words:

Longaville: [*reads*] '*... If by me broke,*[1] *what fool is not so wise*
To lose an oath to win a paradise?'[2]

> [1] *if I break my vow*
> [2] *even a fool would be wise enough to break his word if it meant going to paradise*

Just as Longaville is wondering how to deliver his sonnet to Maria, yet another lone figure arrives on the scene. It is Dumaine, the final member of the group of oath-takers. Longaville hurriedly finds a hiding-place.

Dumaine is hopelessly in love with the princess's attendant Katherine, and wishes they could be together. The others, unseen, echo his desire:

Dumaine: O most divine Kate!
Berowne: [*aside*] O most profane coxcomb![1]
Dumaine: ... O that I had my wish!
Longaville: [*aside*] And I had mine!
King: [*aside*] And I mine too, good Lord!
Berowne: [*aside*] Amen, so[2] I had mine!

> [1] *irreverent fool*
> [2] *as long as*

Dumaine, like the others, has written a poem to express his heartache, and decides to read it aloud. Berowne, who is beginning to tire of poetic outpourings, is unenthusiastic:

Dumaine: I would [1] forget her, but a fever she
            Reigns in my blood, and will remembered be. [2]
Berowne: [*aside*] A fever in your blood? Why then, incision
            Would let her out in saucers. [3] Sweet misprision! [4]
Dumaine: Once more I'll read the ode that I have writ.
Berowne: [*aside*] Once more I'll mark how love can vary wit. [5]

[1] *wish I could*
[2] *she has control over me, like a fever in my blood,
    and forces me to keep her in mind*
[3] *a surgeon could cut open a vein to let her trickle out*
[4] *error, misguided comparison*
[5] *I'll observe how love can lead to folly in a normally
    sensible person*

The oath he has taken, Dumaine laments, is cruel and unnatural for a young man:

Dumaine: [*reads*] 'On a day – alack [1] the day! –
            Love, whose month is ever [2] May,
            Spied a blossom passing fair [3]
            Playing in the wanton [4] air.
            ... But, alack, my hand is sworn
            Ne'er to pluck thee from thy thorn.
            Vow, alack, for youth unmeet,
            Youth so apt to pluck a sweet.' [5]

[1] *alas*
[2] *always*
[3] *exceptionally beautiful*
[4] *lively, playful*
[5] *the vow is inappropriate for a young man, like me,
    who naturally wants to meet a sweetheart*

A fever in your blood? Why then, incision
Would let her out in saucers.

Bloodletting – also known as venesection – was standard medical practice in Shakespeare's day, as it had been for centuries. Doctors would use special instruments to cut open veins, and a measuring bowl to ensure that the correct quantity of blood was removed.

John Hall, a physician who married Shakespeare's daughter Susanna in 1607, frequently carried out bloodletting (even, on occasion, on himself). As his case notes reveal, the treatment was not always popular with patients. One 42-year-old gentleman, suffering from a severe sore throat, swollen tongue and high fever, accepted an enema, a mouthwash, a cough medicine and a poultice, but initially drew the line at bloodletting:

"I prescribed venesection but he refused. I feared his imminent death. He fell into a continual burning fever as I foretold ... Day by day the fever increased, his strength was destroyed, and he declared that he could not survive. He sent me a message on a hard-ridden horse ... After the message reached me, I found him in danger of death, unable to say anything. Immediately I cut a vein and bled to 10 ounces. His voice returned, and he said that he found great relief in the venesection ... That night was more peaceful than others ... He recovered well, by God's will."

John Hall, *A Little Book of Cures, Described in Case Histories and Empirically Proven, Tried and Tested in Certain Places and on Noted People*, 1611–35

Dumaine resolves to send his poem to Katherine, along with a simple declaration of his love. If only the king and the other courtiers were in the same situation, he remarks, he would not feel so guilty:

Dumaine: This will I send, and something else more plain,
            That shall express my true love's fasting[1] pain.
            O, would[2] the King, Berowne, and Longaville
            Were lovers too! Ill, to example ill,
            Would from my forehead wipe a perjured note,[3]
            For none offend where all alike do dote.[4]

        [1] *hungering, yearning*
        [2] *I wish*
        [3] *their bad behaviour would set a precedent, and my
            offence would be erased from the record*
        [4] *if we were all pursuing loved ones, no individual
            could accuse another of breaking his vow*

Passing judgement

Longaville now steps boldly out of his hiding-place, and immediately scolds his companion for breaking the vow that they have all taken. If he had been overheard talking of love in the same way, claims Longaville self-righteously, he would be ashamed:

Longaville: [*comes out of hiding*] Dumaine, thy love is far from
              charity,
            That in love's grief desirest society.[1]
            You may look pale, but I should blush, I know,
            To be o'erheard and taken napping so.[2]

        [1] *it's very mean-spirited of you to wish that others
            would join you in your suffering*
        [2] *if I were caught confessing such things*

The king now emerges from hiding. Longaville realises, to his horror, that his own declaration of love for Maria was overheard. The king is outraged that Longaville should criticise Dumaine for the same offence that Longaville himself has committed:

King: [*comes out of hiding*] Come, sir, you blush! As his, your
        case is such; [1]
    You chide at him, offending twice as much. [2]
    You do not love Maria?

    [1] *you are guilty of the same offence as him*
    [2] *the fact that you condemn Dumaine makes your crime
       twice as bad*

The two men hang their heads in shame as the king sarcastically
repeats their secret revelations:

King: I have been closely shrouded [1] in this bush,
    And marked you both, and for you both did blush.
    I heard your guilty rhymes, observed your fashion, [2]
    Saw sighs reek [3] from you, noted well your passion …
    [*to Longaville*] You would for paradise break faith
       and troth; [4]
    [*to Dumaine*] And Jove, for your love, would infringe
       an oath. [5]

    [1] *secretly hidden*
    [2] *behaviour*
    [3] *emanate, emerge*
    [4] *you were ready to go back on your word in order to
       get to heaven*
    [5] *your love was powerful enough to make Jove himself
       break his oath*

When Berowne hears how the two courtiers have violated their
oaths, the king warns them, they will never hear the end of it:

King: What will Berowne say when that he shall hear
    Faith infringed, which such zeal did swear? [1]
    How will he scorn, how will he spend [2] his wit!
    How will he triumph, leap and laugh at it!
    For all the wealth that ever I did see,
    I would not have him know so much by me. [3]

    [1] *when he hears that your vows, so eagerly sworn,
       have been broken*
    [2] *employ; continue to use until it is exhausted*
    [3] *I wouldn't want him to know such things about me;
       I wouldn't like to be in your shoes*

Savouring the moment

This is Berowne's opportunity to gloat over his companions, and he seizes it gleefully. He emerges triumphantly from his hiding-place and sternly rebukes the three men. The king, in particular, should be ashamed of his condemnation of the two courtiers, as he is every bit as guilty.

Apologising that it should be necessary to criticise the monarch, Berowne reminds him of his sonnet describing the endless tears caused by his love for the French princess:

Berowne: [*comes out of hiding*] Now step I forth to whip[1] hypocrisy.
Ah, good my liege,[2] I pray thee pardon me.
Good heart, what grace hast thou, thus to reprove
These worms for loving, that art most in love?[3]
Your eyes do make no coaches; in your tears
There is no certain Princess that appears.

[1] *expose, punish*
[2] *lord, ruler*
[3] *what right do you have to reprimand these wretches
   for falling in love, when you yourself are infatuated?*

Warming to his theme, Berowne berates all three men at length, and teases them about their supposed heartache:

Berowne: O, what a scene of foolery have I seen,
Of sighs, of groans, of sorrow, and of teen![1]
O me, with what strict patience have I sat,
To see a king transformed to a gnat![2]
… Where lies thy grief? O, tell me, good Dumaine.
And, gentle Longaville, where lies thy pain?
And where my liege's? All about the breast?
A caudle, ho![3]

[1] *grief, lamentation*
[2] *reduced to triviality*
[3] *someone bring some medicine!*

The king is mortified to find that his love for the princess has been revealed. Berowne loftily declares that his friends have let him down. He is the only one still faithful to their solemn oath:

King:	Too bitter is thy jest.
	Are we betrayed thus to thy over-view?[1]
Berowne:	Not you to me, but I betrayed by you;[2]
	I that am honest, I that hold it sin
	To break the vow I am engaged in –
	I am betrayed by keeping company
	With men like you, men of inconstancy.

[1] *have we all been shown up by your observation of us?*
[2] *I am the one who has been betrayed, by your failure to keep to our vow*

Unlike the others, claims Berowne, he would never be found writing foolish verses or groaning from the agonies of love. While he holds forth on his disdain for the excesses of love, two rustic citizens, Jaquenetta and Costard, approach. The dairymaid is carrying a letter: it is for the attention of the king.

The game is up

Jaquenetta explains that the learned men who read the letter for her told her to hand it to the king. Costard originally gave her the letter, she says, claiming it was from Don Armado.

The king asks Berowne to look through the letter. As soon as he sees it, Berowne is horrified: it is not from Armado, but is his own love-letter, complete with sonnet, that Costard was supposed to deliver to Rosaline. Berowne hurriedly tears up the letter before the king has a chance to read it, but his haste attracts the others' attention. He curses Costard for his incompetence:

King:	[*sees Berowne tearing up the letter*] How now, what is in you?[1] Why dost thou tear it?
Berowne:	A toy,[2] my liege, a toy. Your grace needs not fear it.
Longaville:	It did move him to passion, and therefore let's hear it.
Dumaine:	[*picks up the pieces*] It is Berowne's writing, and here is his name.
Berowne:	[*to Costard*] Ah, you whoreson loggerhead,[3] you were born to do me shame.

[1] *what has come over you?*
[2] *a trifle; nothing important*
[3] *bloody idiot*

As his friends seize upon the fragments of his sonnet, Berowne realises that he cannot hide the truth. He immediately confesses that he, like them, is hopelessly in love. The idea of avoiding female company for three years was doomed from the start, he insists. It is futile to try to oppose the forces of nature:

Berowne:	Sweet lords, sweet lovers, O, let us embrace!
	As true we are as flesh and blood can be.[1]
	The sea will ebb and flow, heaven show his face;[2]
	Young blood doth not obey an old decree.[3]
	We cannot cross the cause why we were born;[4]
	Therefore of all hands must we be forsworn.[5]

[1] *we have gone back on our word because we are human*
[2] *tides must ebb and flow, and the sun will always rise*
[3] *the young cannot be expected to obey a command suitable only for the old*
[4] *we cannot go against the drive to procreate, which caused us all to be born*
[5] *all in all, it's inevitable that we should break our vow*

Costard and Jaquenetta leave, and the four friends discuss the subject of love. The king is surprised to hear that Berowne has fallen in love with Rosaline; Berowne, in turn, is amazed that anyone could fail to be overwhelmed by her beauty. His vivid description does not impress the king, however:

King:	What, did these rent lines[1] show some love of thine?
Berowne:	'Did they?' quoth you! Who sees the heavenly Rosaline
	That, like a rude and savage man of Ind,
	At the first opening of the gorgeous East,
	Bows not his vassal head and, strucken blind,
	Kisses the base ground with obedient breast?[2]
King:	What zeal, what fury hath inspired thee now?
	My love, her mistress, is a gracious moon;
	She, an attending star, scarce seen a light.[3]

[1] *the verses you have just torn up*
[2] *who can set eyes on Rosaline without bowing down in awe and reverence, like a primitive sun-worshipper greeting the new dawn?*
[3] *the princess, whom Rosaline serves, is like the moon, while Rosaline is hardly visible, like a faint star*

Berowne's companions tease him about Rosaline who, with her black hair and dark eyes, does not conform to their conventional ideas of attractiveness. He replies that her natural beauty is preferable to the artificially enhanced looks of other women:

Berowne:	O, if in black my lady's brows be decked,[1]
	It mourns that painting and usurping hair
	Should ravish doters with a false aspect;[2]
	And therefore is she born to make black fair[3] ...
Dumaine:	To look like her are chimney-sweepers black.[4]
Longaville:	And since her time are colliers counted bright.[5]
Berowne:	... Your mistresses dare never come in rain,
	For fear their colours[6] should be washed away.

[1] *if Rosaline's hair and eyebrows are black*
[2] *it is in mourning of the fact that lovers can be misled by false appearances created by cosmetics and wigs*
[3] *she proves that naturally dark looks are also beautiful*
[4] *chimney-sweeps get themselves covered in soot and grime in order to look like her*
[5] *since her arrival, coal-miners are considered attractive*
[6] *artificial colours; make-up*

The verbal wrangling continues, but eventually the four men all agree on one thing: they are in love. The king admits that they must inevitably break their earlier oath, but is determined to find a proper justification for doing so. They all turn to Berowne, the most eloquent of the four:

King:	... leave this chat and, good Berowne, now prove
	Our loving lawful and our faith not torn.[1]
Dumaine:	Ay, marry, there; some flattery for this evil.[2]
Longaville:	O, some authority how to proceed.
	Some tricks, some quillets how to cheat the devil.[3]

[1] *demonstrate that we can fall in love while still keeping our integrity intact*
[2] *some persuasive rhetoric to hide our wrongdoing*
[3] *verbal niceties that will save us from condemnation*

> "I have heard this play described as lyrical and full of elegant
> poetry ... But I do not experience the text as lyrical or courtly. I
> find it laced with testosterone ... the images and metaphors that
> leaven the script reference games, sports, warring and battles,
> hunting and pursuit. In this play, perhaps, the challenge is
> everything – an end in itself. It's all about the game – word games,
> games of disguise and the sport of falling in love. Sport is rough
> and competitive and played to win."
>
> Director Terry Hands on his 1990 production of *Love's
> Labour's Lost* for the Royal Shakespeare Company

Rallying the troops

Scarcely pausing to take breath, Berowne launches into a
lengthy, spirited defence of the pursuit of love. He calls on his
companions to think of themselves as soldiers, and to fight back
against the vows they have taken, which are clearly opposed to
the natural inclinations of youth:

Berowne: Have at you, then, affection's men-at-arms![1]
Consider what you first did swear unto:
To fast, to study, and to see no woman –
Flat[2] treason 'gainst the kingly state of youth.

[1] *come on, love's warriors!*
[2] *blatant, outright*

Their plan to study for three years was fundamentally flawed,
he goes on. Learning from books is slow and laborious, whilst
looking into the eyes of their sweethearts has already proved an
inspiration:

Berowne: ... when would you, my liege, or you, or you,
In leaden contemplation[1] have found out
Such fiery numbers as the prompting eyes
Of beauty's tutors have enriched you with?[2]

[1] *dull, weary study*
[2] *found the ability to write such impassioned verses as
those inspired by your beloved's eyes*

While study only engages the brain, love heightens all the senses:

Berowne: It adds a precious seeing to the eye:
            A lover's eyes will gaze an eagle blind.[1]
            A lover's ear will hear the lowest sound,
            When the suspicious head of theft is stopped.[2]
            Love's feeling is more soft and sensible[3]
            Than are the tender horns of cockled snails.[4]

            [1] *outstare an eagle*
            [2] *when even a thief, alert to the slightest sound, hears
            nothing*
            [3] *sensitive*
            [4] *snails in their shells*

Throughout the ages, Berowne continues, love for women has inspired men to commit acts of courage, to compose music, and to write poetry. To cut themselves off wilfully from this source of inspiration would be senseless:

Berowne: From women's eyes this doctrine[1] I derive:
            They sparkle still the right Promethean fire;[2]
            They are the books, the arts, the academes,
            That show, contain, and nourish all the world,
            Else none at all in aught proves excellent.[3]
            Then fools you were these women to forswear[4] …

            [1] *knowledge, learning*
            [2] *they sparkle like the fire brought down from heaven
            by Prometheus, which first brought about human
            civilisation*
            [3] *without which nothing has any value*
            [4] *renounce, swear to avoid*

Finally, Berowne urges his listeners to abandon their vows and embrace their true natures:

Berowne: Let us once lose our oaths[1] to find ourselves,
            Or else we lose ourselves to keep our oaths.

            [1] *on this occasion, we should forget our oaths*

The king and his courtiers, galvanised by Berowne's speech, decide to act immediately. The French visitors are due to leave soon: to avert their departure, the four men decide to organise a gathering at which each of them will capture the heart of his beloved. Joyous festivities, Berowne promises, will bring about the happy ending they all have in mind:

Berowne: ... revels, dances, masques[1] and merry hours
Forerun[2] fair Love, strewing her way with flowers.

> [1] *masked entertainment*
> [2] *run ahead of, prepare the way for*

An urgent commission   V, i

The schoolmaster Holofernes, the curate Nathaniel and constable Dull have finished their midday meal together. Holofernes, as he had promised, has been holding forth on the subject of poetry. The clergyman praises his friend lavishly:

Nathaniel: I praise God for you, sir. Your reasons[1] at dinner have been sharp and sententious,[2] pleasant without scurrility,[3] witty without affection,[4] audacious without impudency,[5] learned without opinion[6] ...

> [1] *arguments, assertions*
> [2] *astute, wise*
> [3] *vulgarity*
> [4] *clever but not pretentious*
> [5] *bold but not disrespectful*
> [6] *arrogance*

Nathaniel mentions that he spoke recently with Don Armado. Holofernes explains, at length, that he is not an admirer of the Spanish knight. Nathaniel dutifully notes down some of the schoolmaster's more obscure vocabulary:

Holofernes: His humour is lofty,[1] his discourse peremptory[2] ... his gait majestical and his general behaviour vain, ridiculous and thrasonical.[3] He is too picked,[4] too spruce, too affected, too odd, as it were, too peregrinate,[5] as I may call it.

Nathaniel: [*brings out his notebook*] A most singular and choice
epithet.

> [1] *his manner is haughty*
> [2] *he is overbearing in conversation*
> [3] *boastful (referring to Thraso, a pompous old soldier*
> *in a play by the Roman dramatist Terence)*
> [4] *fastidious*
> [5] *refined, keen to show how well-travelled he is (an*
> *adjective invented by Holofernes)*

The Spaniard's misuse of the English language, Holofernes
continues, also irritates him intensely. At this moment, however,
Armado himself appears, along with his pageboy Moth and
Costard. Elaborate greetings are exchanged, but they leave
Moth and Costard unimpressed:

Armado: Men of peace, well encountered.
Holofernes: Most military sir, salutation.
Moth: [*to Costard*] They have been at a great feast of
                      languages and stolen the scraps.
Costard: [*to Moth*] O, they have lived long on the alms-basket[1]
                      of words. I marvel thy master hath not eaten thee for
                      a word, for thou art not so long by the head[2] as
                      honorificabilitudinitatibus. Thou art easier swallowed
                      than a flapdragon.[3]

> [1] *a basket containing scraps of unwanted food for*
> *distribution to the poor*
> [2] *tall*
> [3] *a raisin floating in brandy*

> *... thou art not so long by the head as*
> *honorificabilitudinitatibus.*

Costard's obscure, randomly chosen Latin word (meaning
something like 'by the state of being honoured') is the
longest in Shakespeare. Depending on editorial choices,
Love's Labour's Lost also contains Shakespeare's longest
scene (Act V, scene ii) and longest speech (Berowne's
justification for pursuing love rather than learning at the
end of Act IV).

Armado has some news for the schoolmaster, and he draws him aside from the boisterous teasing of Moth and Costard. He mentions, in his meandering way, that the king has arranged an event for the French visitors this afternoon. Holofernes, despite his earlier comments, is intrigued by the Spaniard's choice of words:

Armado: Arts-man, preambulate.[1] We will be singuled from the barbarous.[2] Do you not educate youth at the charge-house[3] on the top of the mountain?

Holofernes: Or *mons*, the hill.

Armado: At your sweet pleasure, for the mountain.[4]

Holofernes: I do, *sans question*.

Armado: Sir, it is the King's most sweet pleasure and affection to congratulate[5] the Princess at her pavilion, in the posteriors of this day, which the rude multitude call the afternoon.

Holofernes: The 'posterior of the day', most generous sir, is liable, congruent, and measurable[6] for the afternoon.

[1] *walk with me, scholar*
[2] *separate ourselves from the uneducated*
[3] *boarding-school*
[4] *as you wish; use whichever word you want for a mountain*
[5] *greet, pay respects to*
[6] *apt, suitable and fitting*

Armado explains that the king, a close friend of his, has asked for his help. Some form of entertainment is needed for this afternoon's celebrations:

Armado: Some certain special honours it pleaseth his greatness to impart to Armado, a soldier, a man of travel, that hath seen the world – but let that pass. The very all of all[1] is – but, sweet heart, I do implore secrecy – that the King would have me present the Princess – sweet chuck![2] – with some delightful ostentation, or show, or pageant, or antic,[3] or firework.

[1] *essence, substance*
[2] *pet, dearest*
[3] *parade with extravagant costumes*

The schoolmaster and the curate are both known for putting on such performances, says Armado, so his thoughts have naturally turned to them. Holofernes responds enthusiastically. He proposes a grand historical pageant to entertain the French princess:

Armado: Now, understanding that the curate and your sweet self are good at such eruptions and sudden breaking-out of mirth, as it were, I have acquainted you withal,[1] to the end to[2] crave your assistance.

Holofernes: Sir, you shall present before her the Nine Worthies.[3]

[1] *with this matter*
[2] *in order to*
[3] *famous figures from the past*

Holofernes hurries away, eager to cast the various roles and start rehearsals. He urges the constable, who has been observing the proceedings in silence, to join him:

Holofernes: *Via,*[1] goodman Dull! Thou hast spoken no word all this while.

Dull: Nor understood none neither, sir.

[1] *come on; get a move on*

> *"There is more warmth than scorn in Shakespeare's remembrance of the both the schoolmasters and the dullards of his Stratford boyhood. The key to his theatrical magnanimity was his capacity to imagine Holofernes and Dull with equal affection."*
>
> Jonathan Bate, *Soul of the Age*, 2008

Tokens of love V, ii

Since the king and his companions decided to abandon their vows and wholeheartedly pursue their sweethearts, gifts and love-poems have started to arrive for the French princess and her ladies-in-waiting.

The princess has received a miniature portrait in a diamond-studded frame from the king, along with copious verses:

Princess:	Sweet hearts, we shall be rich ere we depart,
	If fairings[1] come thus plentifully in.
	A lady walled about[2] with diamonds!
	Look you, what I have from the loving King.
Rosaline:	Madam, came nothing else along with that?
Princess:	Nothing but this? Yes, as much love in rhyme
	As would be crammed up in a sheet of paper,
	Writ o'both sides the leaf, margin and all …

[1] *gifts*
[2] *surrounded, encircled*

The three other women compare the love-tokens they have received: Rosaline has a portrait of herself, drawn by Berowne; Katherine, a pair of gloves from Dumaine; and Maria a string of pearls from Longaville.

Like the princess, each of them has also received a poem from their suitors, but the verses leave them cold. Berowne's is grossly exaggerated in its praise for Rosaline. Katherine finds Dumaine's verses inept and foolish, while Maria considers Longaville's attempt far too long:

Princess:	… Katherine, what was sent to you from fair Dumaine?
Katherine:	Madam, this glove.
Princess:	Did he not send you twain?[1]
Katherine:	Yes, madam, and moreover
	Some thousand verses of a faithful lover.
	A huge translation of hypocrisy,
	Vilely compiled, profound simplicity.[2]
Maria:	This, and these pearls, to me sent Longaville.
	The letter is too long by half a mile.

Princess: I think no less.[3] Dost thou not wish in heart
              The chain were longer and the letter short?

> [1] *a pair*
> [2] *a great pack of lies, clumsy and meaningless*
> [3] *I agree*

All four women are determined to mock their suitors for their sudden transformation from supposedly studious, abstinent scholars to passionate lovers. Rosaline, in particular, intends to get the better of Berowne:

Princess: We are wise girls to mock our lovers so.
Rosaline: They are worse fools to purchase mocking so.[1]
              That same Berowne I'll torture ere I go.
              O, that I knew he were but in by th'week![2]
              How I would make him fawn, and beg, and seek,
              And wait the season, and observe the times,[3]
              And spend his prodigal wits in bootless rhymes,[4]
              And shape his service wholly to my hests[5] ...

> [1] *the fact that they have paid for their mockery with*
>   *these poems and gifts makes them even bigger fools*
> [2] *I wish I could be sure that he is completely ensnared*
> [3] *wait until the time is right, and keep to the rules*
> [4] *waste his talent writing ineffectual poetry*
> [5] *devote himself utterly to my wishes*

They all agree that there is something particularly ludicrous in the spectacle of a normally intelligent man behaving foolishly, particularly under the influence of love:

Princess: None are so surely caught,[1] when they are catched,
              As wit[2] turned fool ...
Maria: Folly in fools bears not so strong a note[3]
              As foolery in the wise when wit doth dote[4] ...

> [1] *utterly captivated*
> [2] *someone with intelligence*
> [3] *doesn't deserve to be blamed as much*
> [4] *when their good judgement descends into folly*

Turning the tables

Lord Boyet now approaches, helpless with laughter. He has been secretly observing the antics of the king and his courtiers, he explains, and has come to warn the women that their four admirers are on their way.

The men intend to approach in disguise, and have persuaded young Moth to act as their herald, announcing their arrival with a grandiose speech. In their bizarre costumes, they will then approach their sweethearts and declare their love. Even if the women are masked, each man will recognise his sweetheart from the love-token she wears:

Princess: But what, but what, come they to visit us?
Boyet: They do, they do, and are apparelled thus,
Like Muscovites, or Russians, as I guess.
Their purpose is to parley, court,[1] and dance,
And every one his love-suit[2] will advance
Unto his several[3] mistress, which they'll know
By favours several which they did bestow.[4]

[1] *converse, flirt*
[2] *plea, declaration of love*
[3] *respective, his own*
[4] *by the gifts that each man gave his beloved*

The princess comes up with a plan at once. They are all to keep their masks on while the men are present and, to confuse their admirers, will exchange their love-tokens with one another:

Princess: The gallants shall be tasked:[1]
For, ladies, we will every one be masked,
And not a man of them shall have the grace,
Despite of suit,[2] to see a lady's face.
Hold, Rosaline, this favour thou shalt wear,
And then the King will court thee for his dear.
Hold, take thou this, my sweet, and give me thine,
So shall Berowne take me for Rosaline.

[1] *tested, challenged*
[2] *none of them will be allowed, despite their pleas*

The princess exchanges gifts with Rosaline, and tells Katherine and Maria to do the same. When Katherine questions her, the princess replies that she wants to counter the men's trickery with a subterfuge of her own:

Katherine: But in this changing what is your intent?
Princess: The effect of my intent is to cross[1] theirs.
            They do it but in mockery merriment,[2]
            And mock for mock[3] is only my intent.
            Their several counsels they unbosom shall
            To loves mistook,[4] and so be mocked withal
            Upon the next occasion that we meet ...

[1] *thwart, confound*
[2] *they are just amusing themselves*
[3] *making fun of their game*
[4] *they will all make their heartfelt declarations of love to the wrong woman*

As well as remaining masked, the princess tells her attendants, they must refuse to dance, and must turn away as soon as the herald's speech begins.

A cool reception

A trumpet sounds, and Moth enters, followed by the four heavily disguised suitors. The young boy has only just started his address when he slips up, distracted at his reception by the French party. Berowne scolds him for forgetting his lines:

Moth: All hail, the richest beauties on the earth!
          ... A holy parcel of the fairest dames
          [*the ladies turn their backs*]
          That ever turned their – backs – to mortal views.
Berowne: Their eyes, villain, their eyes!
Moth: That ever turned their eyes to mortal views.

Eventually Moth gives up, complaining that his audience is ignoring him, and Berowne dismisses him angrily. Rosaline, taking the role of the princess and wearing her diamond-studded brooch, steps forward and addresses the visitors imperiously. With extreme formality, she instructs Boyet to act as go-between:

Rosaline:	What would these strangers?[1] Know their minds, Boyet.
	If they do speak our language, 'tis our will
	That some plain man recount their purposes.
	Know what they would.
Boyet:	What would you with the princess?
Berowne:	Nothing but peace and gentle visitation.[2]
Rosaline:	What would they, say they?
Boyet:	Nothing but peace and gentle visitation.

[1] *what do these foreigners want?*
[2] *a friendly visit, a courtesy call*

They have had their visit, declares Rosaline, so may take their leave now. Boyet again passes on the message. The king now speaks: they have travelled many miles, he claims. Their only aim is to meet the French princess and her attendants, and to dance with them.

Rosaline, still playing the part of the princess, quibbles with the visitors: how many miles have they travelled? How many inches? How many steps? They do not count such things, says Berowne devotedly, begging for at least a sight of their beloveds' faces:

Berowne:	We number[1] nothing that we spend for you.
	Our duty is so rich, so infinite,
	That we may do it still without account.[2]
	Vouchsafe to show the sunshine of your face,
	That we, like savages,[3] may worship it.

[1] *keep count of*
[2] *we are willing to serve you for ever without counting the cost*
[3] *sun-worshipping pagans*

> *Vouchsafe to show the sunshine of your face ...*
>
> *"One of the most pervasive comparisons in lyric and dramatic poetry of the time likened men to the sun and women to the moon. This tradition represented men as constant and women as changeable; men were supposed to provide illumination, while women only borrowed that illumination. But in* Love's Labor's Lost, *the men's praise compares the women almost exclusively to the sun ... Upending the poetic status quo, the inconstant, perjured men change with the moon, breaking their holy vows and wooing the wrong women."*
>
> Akiva Fox, *Trading Places*, Shakespeare Theatre Company, 2006

The women resolutely keep their faces covered. The king then asks for one dance, however brief it may be. His hopes are raised as the princess – so he thinks – tells the musicians to strike up, and offers her hand. She changes her mind a moment later, however, instructing her attendants to offer nothing more than a curtsy:

Rosaline:	Since you are strangers, and come here by chance,
	We'll not be nice.[1] Take hands. We will not dance.
King:	Why take we hands then?
Rosaline:	Only to part friends.
	Curtsy, sweet hearts, and so the measure[2] ends.
	[*the music stops*]

[1] *fastidious, choosy*
[2] *dance*

Eventually Rosaline agrees to a private conversation. The king eagerly accepts, and steps aside with the woman he believes to be his beloved. Berowne now takes the opportunity to approach his own sweetheart, not realising that the woman wearing his gift is the princess. The two of them also wander away for an intimate discussion, and the remaining mismatched couples follow suit.

Boyet watches with amusement as the four lovers, in their outlandish disguises, attempt unsuccessfully to win the women's favour. Finally Rosaline calls an end to the proceedings, and the men make a bad-tempered exit:

Rosaline:	Not one word more, my maids. Break off, break off!
Berowne:	By heaven, all dry-beaten with pure scoff! [1]
King:	Farewell, mad wenches. You have simple wits.

> [1] *battered with mockery*

The women now remove their masks, and excitedly discuss their successful prank. All four men, desperate for the approval of their sweethearts, have pledged their eternal love to the wrong woman:

Rosaline:	The king is my love sworn.
Princess:	And quick [1] Berowne hath plighted faith to me.
Katherine:	And Longaville was for my service born.
Maria:	Dumaine is mine as sure as bark on tree.

> [1] *hasty, impatient*

Boyet warns them that the men will be back soon, out of their disguises, and more determined than ever. Rosaline, keen to continue their game, suggests to the princess that they should all pretend to have been fooled by the exotic visitors they have just encountered.

As predicted, the men soon approach once more, no longer in their Russian costumes, and the women hurry into their tent. Boyet remains outside, guarding the entrance.

The humiliation continues

The king asks Boyet if he might be granted an audience with the princess. Boyet replies that he is sure it will be possible, and retires into the tent. Berowne has developed an intense dislike of the French lord, with his smooth manners and elegant speech:

Berowne: This fellow pecks up wit as pigeons peas,[1]
             And utters it again when God doth please.
             He is wit's pedlar [2] ...

             [1] *picks up clever expressions from here and there*
             [2] *salesman, trader*

Berowne finds the man's excessive refinement and unruffled behaviour exasperating:

Berowne: Why, this is he
             That kissed his hand away in courtesy.[1]
             This is the ape of form,[2] Monsieur the Nice,
             That when he plays at tables chides the dice
             In honourable terms.[3]

             [1] *wore out his hand with kissing*
             [2] *unthinking imitator of genteel behaviour*
             [3] *even if he loses when gambling, he rebukes the dice*
                without swearing

Boyet now emerges from the tent with the princess and her ladies-in-waiting. The king announces that he wishes to invite the French delegation to his court. The princess refuses. Inviting women into the royal household would mean breaking his earlier vow, she reminds him, so she would prefer to remain camped out in the parkland:

King: We came to visit you, and purpose now
             To lead you to our court. Vouchsafe[1] it then.
Princess: This field shall hold me, and so hold your vow.[2]
             Nor God nor I delights in perjured men.[3]

             [1] *grant, agree to*
             [2] *I will stay in this field, so that your vow remains*
                unbroken
             [3] *men who have broken their word*

His vow is no longer important, replies the king; and it was her beauty that persuaded him to break it. The princess is unmoved. Vows are important things, she maintains, and she will not be party to his sudden change of heart. The king urges her to escape from the isolation of her present accommodation, but again the princess insists that she will remain where she is. They have not lacked entertainment, she tells the king, who pretends not to understand:

King:	O, you have lived in desolation here,
	Unseen, unvisited, much to our shame.
Princess:	Not so, my lord. It is not so, I swear.
	We have had pastimes here and pleasant game:
	A mess[1] of Russians left us but of late.[2]
King:	How, madam? Russians?

[1] *group*
[2] *not long ago*

To the embarrassment of the king and his friends, it soon becomes clear that the women had recognised them under their Russian disguises. Noticing the king's uneasiness, Rosaline pretends to be sympathetic. Berowne decides that it is time to put an end to their antics and make a clean breast of things. His defences down, he invites Rosaline to speak her mind:

King:	[*aside, to his courtiers*] We were descried.[1] They'll
	mock us now downright.
Princess:	... Amazed, my lord? Why looks your highness sad?
Rosaline:	Help, hold his brows! He'll swoon! Why look you pale?
	Seasick, I think, coming from Muscovy![2]
Berowne:	Thus pour the stars down plagues for perjury.[3]
	Can any face of brass hold longer out?[4]
	Here stand I, lady; dart thy skill at me.
	Bruise me with scorn, confound me with a flout,[5]
	Thrust thy sharp wit quite through my ignorance ...

[1] *found out, spotted*
[2] *Russia*
[3] *this is how the heavens punish us for dishonesty*
[4] *could anyone now be brazen enough to maintain his innocence?*
[5] *destroy me with your mockery*

His deviousness and his witty, overblown language have achieved nothing, Berowne admits. It is time to leave the rhetoric behind:

Berowne: Taffeta phrases, silken terms precise,[1]
           Three-piled hyperboles, spruce affectation,[2]
           Figures pedantical[3] – these summer flies
           Have blown me full of maggot ostentation.[4]
           I do forswear[5] them …

> [1] *expressions that are excessively elaborate and fussy, like fashionable clothing*
> [2] *extravagant statements as rich as expensive velvet, and clever posturing*
> [3] *erudite figures of speech*
> [4] *just as flies leave flesh infested with maggots, all my rhetoric has puffed me up with self-importance*
> [5] *renounce*

From now on, promises Berowne, he will express himself plainly and honestly: and he will start with an open declaration of love for Rosaline. He cannot quite shake off his old habits at once, however:

Berowne: Henceforth my wooing mind shall be expressed
           In russet yeas and honest kersey noes.[1]
           And to begin: wench, so God help me, law![2]
           My love to thee is sound, sans[3] crack or flaw.
Rosaline: Sans 'sans',[4] I pray you.
Berowne: Yet I have a trick
           Of the old rage.[5] Bear with me, I am sick;
           I'll leave it by degrees.[6]

> [1] *in simple language (russet and kersey were types of coarse, homespun cloth)*
> [2] *indeed, truly*
> [3] *without*
> [4] *don't use pretentious French words*
> [5] *I still have a trace of my previous folly*
> [6] *I'll get rid of it gradually*

More broken vows

Berowne urges the women to hear their lovers' pleas; his companions, like him, are suffering just as painfully as if they had been struck down with a terrible disease. He suggests that the women may have similar feelings, as they are wearing the love-tokens sent by their admirers:

Berowne: Write 'Lord have mercy on us' on those three.[1]
They are infected; in their hearts it lies.
They have the plague, and caught it of [2] your eyes.
These lords are visited: you are not free,[3]
For the lords' tokens [4] on you do I see.

[1] *these words were often written on the doors of plague victims' houses*
[2] *from*
[3] *they have caught the disease, and you have not escaped*
[4] *the gifts sent by the four men; also, the 'Lord's tokens' referred to marks that appeared on the skin of those infected with the plague*

They have the plague ...

There are numerous references to the plague in Shakespeare's plays. Throughout his career, the plague frequently resulted in the closure of the London theatres. But it was not only in the capital that the plague cast its shadow; in Shakespeare's home town it had wiped out almost one in six of the population in the course of a few terrible months in 1564. The newborn Shakespeare was lucky to survive unscathed:

"Plague was a frequent and devastating occurrence in England throughout Shakespeare's lifetime. Those who contracted it could suffer from fevers, delirium, and painful plague sores, with a survival rate of just fifty percent. In 1564, the year Shakespeare was born, plague claimed over two hundred people in Stratford-upon-Avon, including four children on his very street."

Holly Kelsey, *Pestilence and Playwright*, 2016

There is no reason to suppose that she or her attendants are in love, retorts the princess: the men gave the gifts of their own free will, and the women are free to choose whether or not to wear them. Berowne, despondent, falls silent. The king, more diplomatic than his friend, now intervenes. He admits that the men, disguised as Russians, tried to court their sweethearts:

King:	Teach us, sweet madam, for our rude transgression [1]
	Some fair excuse.
Princess:	The fairest is confession.
	Were not you here but even now, disguised?
King:	Madam, I was.
Princess:	And were you well advised? [2]
King:	I was, fair madam.
Princess:	When you then were here,
	What did you whisper in your lady's ear?
King:	That more than all the world I did respect [3] her.

[1] *discourteous behaviour, impudence*
[2] *in your right mind*
[3] *esteem, value*

The princess continues with her questioning, asking the king whether he will stand by everything he said to his beloved; after all, he has already broken his earlier oath. The king insists, on his word of honour, that he will keep his promise.

At this point the princess asks Rosaline to step forward and repeat the words that the king, in his disguise, had spoken to her. The princess assures her that the king will keep his word, and playfully offers her best wishes for their future together:

Princess:	Rosaline,
	What did the Russian whisper in your ear?
Rosaline:	Madam, he swore that he did hold me dear
	As precious eyesight, and did value me
	Above this world; adding thereto, moreover,
	That he would wed me or else die my lover. [1]
Princess:	God give thee joy of him! [2] The noble lord
	Most honourably doth uphold his word.

[1] *even if he could not marry me, he would always love me*
[2] *I hope you are happy with him*

The king is appalled: his words of love had been meant for the princess, not Rosaline. Although all the women had been masked, he had recognised the princess as she was wearing his gift, a diamond brooch. The princess casually mentions that, at the time, Rosaline was wearing the brooch. It now dawns on the men that all four of them, deceived by the exchanged love-tokens, have declared their devotion to the wrong woman.

The princess teases Berowne, who, believing her to be Rosaline, had asked for her hand in marriage. He had even given her a pearl, as a further token of his love:

King:	I knew her [1] by this jewel on her sleeve.
Princess:	Pardon me, sir, this jewel did she wear, [2]
	And Lord Berowne, I thank him, is my dear. [3]
	What, will you have me, or your pearl again? [4]
Berowne:	Neither of either; I remit both twain. [5]

[1] *I recognised the princess*
[2] *Rosaline was wearing the brooch*
[3] *has declared his love for me*
[4] *do you want to marry me, or do you want your pearl back?*
[5] *I give up both things*

Boyet and the French ladies are delighted at their success in embarrassing the four lovesick men. Berowne, feeling thoroughly defeated, is convinced that someone found out about their plan to visit the women in disguise and reported it to the princess:

Berowne:	I see the trick on't. [1] Here was a consent, [2]
	Knowing aforehand of our merriment,
	To dash it like a Christmas comedy. [3]
	Some carry-tale, some please-man, some slight zany,
	Some mumble-news [4] ...

[1] *I can see the prank that they've played*
[2] *plot, agreement*
[3] *to ruin it and turn it into a pantomime*
[4] *tell-tale, sycophant, feeble clown, gossip*

Berowne turns angrily to Boyet, who is clearly enjoying the men's discomfort. His furious rant at the French lord soon fizzles out, however, and to his relief another visitor appears on the scene: it is Costard, and he has an important request for the assembled nobility.

The actors await

Costard informs the gathering that the pageant of the Nine Worthies, under the direction of the schoolmaster Holofernes, is ready for performance. His message is garbled and illogical, but he eventually makes his point, adding modestly that he is to act in the pageant himself:

Berowne:	Welcome, pure wit, thou partest a fair fray.[1]
Costard:	O lord, sir, they would know [2]
	Whether the three Worthies shall come in or no.
Berowne:	What, are there but three?
Costard:	No, sir, but it is vara fine,[3]
	For every one pursents [4] three.
Berowne:	And three times thrice is nine.
Costard:	Not so, sir, under correction, sir, I hope it is not so.
Berowne:	… By Jove, I always took three threes for nine.
Costard:	O Lord, sir, it were pity you should get your living by reckoning,[5] sir.
Berowne:	How much is it?
Costard:	O Lord, sir, the parties themselves, the actors, sir, will show whereuntil it doth amount. For mine own part, I am, as they say, but to perfect one man in one poor man – Pompion [6] the Great, sir.

[1] *you're breaking up quite a fight*
[2] *the others would like to know*
[3] *it's perfectly all right*
[4] *represents, depicts*
[5] *it would be hard for you if you had to make a living from arithmetic*
[6] *pumpkin; Costard means 'Pompey'*

They are all ready to see the show, Berowne tells him, and Costard hurries off to join his fellow actors. The king is uneasy at the impression the amateur dramatics will make on his guests, but Berowne shrugs off his concern. They have already made fools of themselves, he points out, with their attempt to disguise themselves as Russians. With luck, this pageant will make them look slightly less ludicrous in comparison:

> *King:*   Berowne, they will shame us. Let them not approach.
> *Berowne:* We are shame-proof, my lord; and 'tis some policy [1]
>   To have one show worse than the King's and his
>   company. [2]
>
> [1] *a good strategy*
> [2] *worse than our own*

The princess, overhearing their conversation, insists that the pageant should go ahead, however bad it is. The earnest efforts of the performers are likely to prove hilarious, despite their serious subject-matter:

> *Princess:* Nay, my good lord, let me o'errule you now.
>   That sport best pleases that doth least know how [1] –
>   Where zeal strives to content, and the contents
>   Dies in the zeal of that which it presents; [2]
>   Their form confounded makes most form in mirth,
>   When great things labouring perish in their birth. [3]
>
> [1] *the best performances are those that are*
>   *unintentionally funny*
> [2] *when, desperate to please, the actors manage to*
>   *ruin the contents of their performance with their*
>   *enthusiasm*
> [3] *the failure of their efforts makes the best*
>   *entertainment, and their ambitious enterprise is*
>   *doomed from the start*

Don Armado now approaches, and presents the king with a description of the planned entertainment. He confides to the king that he is anxious about the performance of the schoolmaster Holofernes; according to Armado, the man is vain and ridiculous. He promises, nevertheless, that they will do their best in their presentation of the Nine Worthies.

The king looks through Armado's list. The Spaniard himself is to present Hector of Troy, a mythological warrior prince, hero of the wars between the Greeks and the Trojans. Costard will play Pompey the Great, the renowned general and statesman of ancient Rome. Nathaniel the clergyman is cast as the commander and conqueror Alexander the Great. The diminutive Moth, Armado's pageboy, is to represent Hercules, and Holofernes has taken the part of Judas Maccabeus, a hero of the Old Testament who led a Jewish rebellion against a mighty Asiatic empire.

A postscript to Armado's note mentions the remaining Worthies, although there is confusion over the numbers involved:

King:	[reads] '... And if these four Worthies in their first show thrive, These four will change habits [1] and present the other five.'
Berowne:	There is five in the first show.
King:	You are deceived: 'tis not so.
Berowne:	The pedant, the braggart, the hedge-priest, the fool and the boy. [2]

[1] clothes, costumes
[2] Holofernes, Armado, Nathaniel, Costard and Moth

The king and his courtiers, along with the princess and her attendants, all gather round, ready to watch the show. They are now in high spirits, and are determined, one way or another, to enjoy the performance.

... These four will change habits ...

"The play's concern with numbers might suggest we are on stronger ground with arithmetic than with slippery words ... But this is clearly not always the case, for in the mouths or minds of some of the play's characters numbers too are regularly shown to be arbitrary in their signification."

H. R. Woudhuysen, Introduction to the Arden
Shakespeare edition of *Love's Labour's Lost*, 1998

A lively audience

Costard, in the guise of an ancient Roman, is the first to appear. He presses ahead with his lines despite heckling from the audience, but slips up almost immediately:

Costard:	'I Pompey am, Pompey surnamed the Big – '
Dumaine:	The 'Great'.
Costard:	It is 'Great', sir: 'Pompey surnamed the Great,
	That oft in field, with targe[1] and shield, did make my
	foe to sweat ...'

[1] *small round shield*

He ends his brief speech with a tribute to the princess, stepping out of character almost immediately to comment on his own performance:

Costard:	'... travelling along this coast, I here am come by chance,
	And lay my arms before the legs of this sweet lass of France.'
	If your ladyship would say 'Thanks, Pompey', I had done.
Princess:	Great thanks, Great Pompey.
Costard:	'Tis not so much worth,[1] but I hope I was perfect.[2]
	I made a little fault in 'Great'.

[1] *it wasn't that good*
[2] *word perfect*

Costard steps to one side and the clergyman Nathaniel enters, attired as a warrior. He announces himself as Alexander the Great, but is almost immediately reduced to a nervous silence by the rowdy audience. Berowne calls for him to be removed:

Berowne:	Pompey the Great –
Costard:	Your servant, and Costard.
Berowne:	Take away the conqueror; take away Alisander.
Costard:	[*to Nathaniel*] O sir, you have overthrown[1] Alisander the conqueror ... A conqueror, and afeard to speak? Run away for shame, Alisander.

[1] *dishonoured, disgraced*

Costard ushers Nathaniel off the stage. He explains to the spectators that the curate, although he has many good qualities, has been miscast as Alexander the Great:

Costard: There, an't shall please you,[1] a foolish mild man; an honest man, look you, and soon dashed.[2] He is a marvellous good neighbour, faith, and a very good bowler;[3] but for Alisander, alas, you see how 'tis – a little o'erparted.[4]

[1] *if you please*
[2] *easily discouraged*
[3] *bowls player*
[4] *not quite up to the role he was given*

... a little o'erparted.

The word 'overparted' seems to have been created by Shakespeare to describe an actor struggling with a demanding role. This single word is surprisingly significant. It reflects the fact that Shakespeare had recently become a member (and shareholder) of a theatre company, the Lord Chamberlain's Men: and he was now involved in the practical business of putting on plays – such as casting actors in suitable roles – in addition to his acting and writing duties.

Most playwrights of the time would be paid a set fee for each play, and would have little or no involvement in its production. Shakespeare, by contrast, now had a close working relationship with a stable company of actors who performed his plays. This relationship, unique in its day, was to prove hugely successful for Shakespeare and for the company as a whole:

"He invented a new role for himself, that of in-house company dramatist. Where his peers and predecessors had to sell their plays to the theatre managers on a poorly-paid piecework basis, Shakespeare took a percentage of the box-office income ... by holding shares, he was effectively earning himself a royalty on his work, something no author had ever done before in England."

Jonathan Bate, *Shakespeare's Career in the Theatre*, 2008

The princess asks Costard to step aside and make way for the next act. Holofernes then enters, along with Moth. The schoolmaster introduces the boy, who is holding a club and grappling with a toy snake:

Holofernes: 'Great Hercules is presented by this imp,
Whose club killed Cerberus,[1] that three-headed *canus*,[2]
And when he was a babe, a child, a shrimp,
Thus did he strangle serpents in his *manus*.'[3]

[1] *ferocious three-headed dog of the underworld*
[2] *dog (Holofernes means 'canis')*
[3] *hand*

The boy then makes his exit, and Holofernes proclaims his own character, Judas Maccabeus. However, he is immediately interrupted by the audience, who deliberately mistake him for Judas Iscariot, the disciple who betrayed Jesus Christ and later killed himself out of remorse:

Holofernes: 'Judas I am – '
Dumaine: The more shame for you, Judas.
Holofernes: What mean you, sir?
Boyet: To make Judas hang himself.

The relentless barracking continues, and Holofernes eventually gives up and leaves the stage. The princess feels a pang of sympathy for the unhappy schoolmaster:

Boyet: … as he is an ass, let him go.
              And so adieu, sweet Jude. Nay, why dost thou stay?
Dumaine: For the latter end of his name.
Berowne: For the 'ass' to the Jude? Give it him. Jud-ass, away!
Holofernes: This is not generous, not gentle, not humble.
Boyet: A light for Monsieur Judas! It grows dark, he may
              stumble. [*Holofernes leaves*]
Princess: Alas, poor Maccabeus, how hath he been baited![1]

[1] *persecuted, attacked*

> *This is not generous, not gentle, not humble.*
>
> *"The Nine Worthies are a pantheon of heroes from the classical, Hebrew and Christian eras and, as such, are models for Navarre's courtiers to emulate. But there is no evidence that they are conscious of this: their 'wit' is all bent on making fun of the players rather than taking on board the import of their show ... For once, Holofernes' every word strikes home. The courtiers are, in every sense, forgetting themselves, frustrating the tableau's aim of reminding them who they might be."*
>
> Richard Dutton, *William Shakespeare: A Literary Life*, 1989

A fighter brought down

Don Armado now makes a grand entrance as the warrior Hector. Undaunted by the heckling, he presses on with his bombastic speech:

Armado: 'The armipotent[1] Mars, of lances the almighty,
Gave Hector a gift, the heir of Ilion;[2]
A man so breathed[3] that certain he would fight, yea,
From morn till night, out of his pavilion.'[4]

[1] *strong in battle*
[2] *son of the King of Troy*
[3] *vigorous, in good condition*
[4] *tent, encampment*

Armado appeals to the audience to show respect for the long-dead Hector. The princess assures him that he has their attention:

Armado: The sweet war-man is dead and rotten. Sweet chucks,[1] beat not the bones of the buried. When he breathed, he was a man. But I will forward with my device.[2] Sweet royalty, bestow on me the sense of hearing.
Princess: Speak, brave Hector. We are much delighted.
Armado: I do adore thy grace's slipper.

[1] *dears, darlings*
[2] *press on with my performance*

No sooner has Armado resumed his speech, however, than Costard cuts in with a dramatic announcement about the milkmaid Jaquenetta:

Armado: 'This Hector far surmounted Hannibal;
             The party is gone – '[1]
Costard: Fellow Hector, she is gone! She is two months on her way.
Armado: What meanest thou?
Costard: Faith, unless you play the honest Trojan,[2] the poor
            wench is cast away.[3] She's quick,[4] the child brags in
            her belly already. 'Tis yours.

   [1] *the man in question, Hector, is now dead*
   [2] *do the honourable thing; marry her*
   [3] *ruined*
   [4] *pregnant*

Armado is furious with Costard, and threatens to kill him. To the audience's delight, the two men, still attired as warriors of the ancient world, square up to one another:

Armado: Dost thou infamonise[1] me among potentates?[2] Thou
             shalt die!
Costard: Then shall Hector be whipped for Jaquenetta that is
             quick by him, and hanged for Pompey that is dead
             by him.
Dumaine: Most rare Pompey!
Boyet: Renowned Pompey!
Dumaine: … Hector trembles.
Berowne: Pompey is moved.[3]

   [1] *slander, defame*
   [2] *in this royal company*
   [3] *stirred, roused*

Costard strips down to his shirt, ready to fight. Moth, Armado's page, urges his master to do the same. The Spanish knight, despite his self-proclaimed valour and military expertise, is forced to decline:

Moth: … Do you not see Pompey is uncasing[1] for the combat?
             What mean you? You will lose your reputation.

Armado:	Gentlemen and soldiers, pardon me. I will not combat in my shirt.
Dumaine:	You may not deny it.[2] Pompey hath made the challenge.
Armado:	Sweet bloods, I both may and will.
Berowne:	What reason have you for't?
Armado:	The naked truth of it is, I have no shirt.

[1] *undressing, taking off his outer garments*
[2] *refuse, turn down the challenge*

Armado claims that he goes without the traditional linen undershirt out of religious zeal; the discomfort of outer woollen clothes against his skin is an exercise in devotion and repentance. Moth reveals that the truth is very different: Armado, in reality, lives in shabby poverty. He does not own a shirt.

A serious note

The festivities are brought to a sudden halt by the arrival of a messenger from France, Monsieur Marcadé. The princess quickly realises, from his demeanour, that he brings bad news:

Marcadé:	God save you, madam.
Princess:	Welcome, Marcadé, But[1] that thou interruptest our merriment.
Marcadé:	I am sorry, madam, for the news I bring Is heavy in my tongue. The King, your father –
Princess:	Dead, for my life!
Marcadé:	Even so; my tale is told.[2]

[1] *apart from the fact*
[2] *it is true, and I have nothing else to say*

In many productions, Marcadé is dressed in black to deliver his solemn message:

"His sudden arrival, brief announcement, and immediate fading from view suggest something of the medieval personification of Death itself, coming like a thief in the night."

J. J. Anderson, *The Morality of* Love's Labour's Lost, 1971

The mood changes at once, and Berowne calls for the pageant to be stopped. The princess tells her attendants to prepare for departure; as heiress to the throne, she must return to France as soon as possible.

The king asks the princess to stay, but she gently refuses. She thanks her hosts, admitting that she and her ladies-in-waiting have been rather light-hearted in their dealings with the king and his courtiers:

Princess: Boyet, prepare. I will away tonight.
King: Madam, not so. I do beseech you, stay.
Princess: Prepare, I say. I thank you, gracious lords,
For all your fair endeavours, and entreat,[1]
Out of a new-sad soul, that you vouchsafe [2]
In your rich wisdom to excuse or hide
The liberal opposition of our spirits,[3]
If over-boldly we have borne ourselves
In the converse of breath.[4]

[1] *request*
[2] *agree, grant*
[3] *overlook our wilfulness and lack of restraint*
[4] *if we have been too free and outspoken in our conversations*

As she prepares to leave, the princess expresses her gratitude to the king. The original purpose of her visit, to settle the dispute between France and Navarre, has been accomplished more easily than she had anticipated:

Princess: Farewell, worthy lord.
A heavy heart bears not a nimble tongue.
Excuse me so,[1] coming too short of thanks
For my great suit so easily obtained.[2]

[1] *then, therefore*
[2] *if I have not thanked you enough for willingly granting the important request that brought me here*

The king, anxious for the princess to stay, raises the subject of his feelings for her. This is not the time to talk of marriage, he acknowledges; but his desires and hopes for the future remain the same, and grief and mourning should not hinder the course of love. However, his elegant, poetic words are lost on the unhappy princess:

King: ... though the mourning brow of progeny [1]
                  Forbid the smiling courtesy of love
                  The holy suit which fain it would convince, [2]
                  Yet, since love's argument was first on foot,
                  Let not the cloud of sorrow jostle it
                  From what it purposed [3] ...
Princess: I understand you not. My griefs are double. [4]

       [1] *a child's mourning for the death of a parent*
       [2] *forbids the joyful proposal of marriage which I wish*
          I could make
       [3] *since I have already declared my love, I hope that*
          sorrow will not be allowed to deter it
       [4] *my grief is increased by the fact that I don't*
          understand you

Berowne intervenes. He confesses that the four men have utterly failed to keep to their original promise to spend three years in scholarly seclusion, and have behaved foolishly in their pursuit of the French women:

Berowne: For your fair sakes have we neglected time, [1]
               Played foul play [2] with our oaths. Your beauty, ladies,
               Hath much deformed [3] us, fashioning our humours
               Even to the opposed end of our intents. [4]

       [1] *wasted time, been inattentive*
       [2] *played false, been disloyal*
       [3] *altered*
       [4] *making us become the opposite of what we had*
          intended

These faults, Berowne continues, demonstrate the strength and constancy of the men's feelings; in being false to their vows, they prove themselves true to their loves.

The princess is unsure. She and the other women have regarded the men's attentions as no more than a pleasant diversion, and have responded in the same vein:

Princess: We have received your letters, full of love,
Your favours,[1] the ambassadors of love,
And in our maiden council rated them
At courtship, pleasant jest, and courtesy[2] ...

[1] *gifts*
[2] *in our discussions, we all considered these things to*
be part of an enjoyable, flirtatious game

The men unanimously assert that their pledges of love were genuine and heartfelt. The king makes a final appeal to the women, but the princess brings him down to earth:

Dumaine: Our letters, madam, showed much more than jest.
Longaville: So did our looks.
Rosaline: We did not quote them so.[1]
King: Now, at the latest minute of the hour,
Grant us your loves.
Princess: A time, methinks, too short
To make a world-without-end bargain[2] in.

[1] *that isn't how we interpreted them*
[2] *everlasting vow*

Twelve months of adversity

Although the princess cannot agree to the king's last-minute plea, she does not reject him outright. She challenges him to spend a year in lonely contemplation:

Princess: Your oath I will not trust; but go with speed
To some forlorn and naked[1] hermitage,
Remote from all the pleasures of the world.
There stay until the twelve celestial signs
Have brought about the annual reckoning.

[1] *abandoned, unfurnished*

If the king's love for her can survive such an arduous year of isolation and discomfort, the princess promises, she will be his.

She takes his hand:

Princess: If this austere insociable life
             Change not your offer made in heat of blood;
             If frosts and fasts, hard lodging, and thin weeds [1]
             Nip not the gaudy blossoms of your love,[2]
             But that it bear this trial and last love; [3]
             Then, at the expiration of the year,
             Come challenge me, challenge me by these deserts,[4]
             And, by this virgin palm now kissing thine,
             I will be thine.

[1] *difficult living conditions and inadequate clothing*
[2] *do not cause this bright flowering of your love to wither and die*
[3] *your love withstands this test and remains true*
[4] *come and claim what you have deserved*

Whatever the king decides to do, the princess tells him, she herself will spend the year in mourning for her dead father. The king accepts her proposal without hesitation. He will gladly endure a year of self-denial and suffering for her sake:

King: If this, or more than this, I would deny,
          To flatter up these powers of mine with rest,[1]
          The sudden hand of death close up mine eye!
          Hence, hermit, then.[2] My heart is in thy breast.

[1] *if I refuse your challenge, and choose instead to pamper myself with an easy life*
[2] *from this point onwards I will become a hermit*

> *"As with most of Shakespeare's comedies,* Love's Labor's Lost *has its share of mistaken identities, mis-delivered love letters, self-deluded egoists, songs and clowning. Yet there is a lovely sense of vulnerability and caring beneath the sometimes raucous outer shell of silliness, games, one-upmanship, disguise, outrageousness and role-playing."*
>
> D. Scott Glasser, Director's notes on the Nebraska Shakespeare Festival production of *Love's Labour's Lost,* 2007

As the two of them wander away, deep in conversation, Dumaine approaches his beloved Katherine. She light-heartedly brushes aside his earnest request, hinting that he is still rather immature:

Dumaine: But what to me, my love? But what to me?
            A wife?
Katherine: A beard, fair health, and honesty;
            With threefold love I wish you all these three.

For the present, Katherine tells Dumaine, she is not interested in hearing flattering words of love. However, she suggests that Dumaine should accompany the king when he comes to France in a year's time; she may then be open to persuasion. She warns her suitor not to make any promises, as he has already broken his word once:

Katherine: A twelvemonth and a day
            I'll mark no words that smooth-faced wooers say.[1]
            Come when the King doth to my lady come;
            Then, if I have much love, I'll give you some.
Dumaine: I'll serve thee true and faithfully till then.
Katherine: Yet swear not, lest ye be forsworn again.[2]

> [1] *I'll take no notice of anyone who approaches me with sycophantic words of love*
> [2] *in case you break your oath a second time*

Longaville now approaches Maria. She too will observe the long period of mourning for the French king, but hopes to be united with her admirer when the year is over:

Longaville: What says Maria?
Maria: At the twelvemonth's end
            I'll change my black gown for a faithful friend.[1]
Longaville: I'll stay[2] with patience, but the time is long.
Maria: The liker you; few taller are so young.[3]

> [1] *I'll exchange my mourning clothes for a faithful lover*
> [2] *wait*
> [3] *that's just like you; few men are as upright and honourable as you, even though you are young*

An appeal for compassion

Maria steps aside with Longaville. Now that the three couples are absorbed in each other's company, Berowne is left alone with Rosaline, who appears to be lost in thought. He asks her to look into his eyes, and to demand whatever she wants of him. In response, she first describes his reputation as a man who is unsparing in his mockery and his cutting remarks:

Rosaline: Oft have I heard of you, my lord Berowne,
            Before I saw you, and the world's large tongue
            Proclaims you for a man replete with mocks,[1]
            Full of comparisons and wounding flouts,[2]
            Which you on all estates will execute
            That lie within the mercy of your wit.[3]

> [1] *you are widely renowned for your scathing wit*
> [2] *derisive comments and hurtful gibes*
> [3] *which you inflict remorselessly on people of all kinds*

Berowne's pitiless exercise of his verbal skill is not a quality that Rosaline finds attractive. She has a proposal that will encourage him to use his wit and his intelligence for a more humane purpose:

Rosaline: To weed this wormwood[1] from your fruitful brain,
            And therewithal to win me, if you please,[2]
            Without the which I am not to be won,
            You shall this twelvemonth term from day to day
            Visit the speechless sick and still[3] converse
            With groaning wretches ...

> [1] *eradicate the bitterness*
> [2] *thereby win my love, if that is what you want*
> [3] *continually, regularly*

Rosaline challenges Berowne to bring comfort, through humour and sympathy, to those who are gravely ill and living in pain. Berowne argues that she has asked him to do the impossible, but Rosaline insists that it will teach him to rid himself of his uncaring sarcasm. He has become too used to the easy laughter of his like-minded companions, she suggests:

Rosaline: … your task shall be
            With all the fierce endeavour of your wit
            To enforce the pained impotent [1] to smile.
Berowne: To move wild laughter in the throat of death?
            It cannot be, it is impossible.
            Mirth cannot move a soul in agony.
Rosaline: Why, that's the way to choke a gibing spirit,
            Whose influence is begot of that loose grace
            Which shallow laughing hearers give to fools. [2]

[1] *those who have been rendered helpless and feeble through pain*
[2] *this is how you can overcome your inclination to mock people, which has been encouraged by the unthinking approval of those who are ready to laugh at anything*

"… the ever sportive and witty ladies do not sport about marriage. The ladies are never more grounded, more insightful or more honest than at the play's end, when they treat the serious matter of marriage seriously, not as the hormone rush that the lords are experiencing."

Dr Susan Willis, *Live and Learn: The Pursuit of Worthiness*, 2005

Rosaline urges Berowne to give more consideration to others, not simply to indulge in witticisms for his own pleasure:

Rosaline: A jest's prosperity [1] lies in the ear
                Of him that hears it, never in the tongue
                Of him that makes it.

            [1] *success, enjoyment*

When he visits the sick and the distressed, perhaps Berowne's cruel, courtly wit will be appreciated; if that is the case, says Rosaline, she will take him as he is. It is far more likely, however, that he will succeed if he abandons his cynicism, a prospect that she relishes:

Rosaline: … if sickly ears,
                Deafed [1] with the clamours of their own dear [2] groans,
                Will hear your idle scorns, [3] continue then,
                And I will have you and that fault withal; [4]
                But if they will not, throw away that spirit,
                And I shall find you empty of that fault,
                Right joyful of your reformation.

            [1] *deafened*
            [2] *grievous, dire*
            [3] *cynical sneering*
            [4] *along with that flaw in your character*

Berowne stoically accepts Rosaline's challenge:

Berowne: A twelvemonth? Well, befall what will befall, [1]
                I'll jest a twelvemonth in an hospital.

            [1] *whatever will happen will happen; I'll let events take their course*

A delayed ending

The other couples, in the meantime, have been exchanging their final fond words before their year-long separation. The princess and the king now rejoin Berowne, who remarks that their courtship has not ended in the traditional manner. If the French ladies had been more compliant, he complains, four weddings would now be imminent. The king assures him that they will all have their happy ending eventually, but Berowne is less patient:

Berowne:	Our wooing doth not end like an old play:
	Jack hath not Jill. These ladies' courtesy [1]
	Might well have made our sport a comedy. [2]
King:	Come, sir, it wants [3] a twelvemonth and a day,
	And then 'twill end.
Berowne:	That's too long for a play.

[1] *if the ladies had behaved more conventionally*
[2] *our efforts might have ended in marriage, just as they would in a comedy*
[3] *the waiting will last*

A familiar figure now appears: it is Don Armado, last seen as Hector of Troy, who had left the stage in disgrace, threatened by Costard and embarrassed by the revelation of his financial difficulties. His spirits have now recovered completely, and he announces proudly that the milkmaid Jaquenetta has agreed to be his. She, like the other women, has imposed her own conditions, and he will need to toil long and hard for her love:

Armado:	I am a votary; [1] I have vowed to Jaquenetta to hold the plough [2] for her sweet love three year.

[1] *I have taken a sacred oath; I am a devotee*
[2] *work on the land, become a farmer*

Armado mentions that their pageant, which was brought to an untimely end by the arrival of the news from France, has not quite finished: the two learned men, Holofernes and Nathaniel, have composed a song to bring their show to a close. The song consists of a dialogue between the owl and the cuckoo, he explains. The king is keen to hear it, and Armado calls for the performers to return to the stage.

Earlier mistakes, disputes and humiliations are forgotten as the remaining players join the royal party. Holofernes and Nathaniel return, along with Costard and young Moth, Armado's pageboy. Jaquenetta, now betrothed to Armado, also appears, as does the taciturn constable Dull.

In 1592, when Shakespeare was twenty-eight, he was starting to make a name for himself in the London theatre world as an actor and playwright. In the summer of that year, however, the capital was struck by the worst outbreak of plague in the whole of Elizabeth's reign, leading to hundreds of deaths every month.

London's theatres, already closed due to widespread riots over the price of food, were forced to remain shut for another two years. Some theatre companies were disbanded, while others left London and tried to make a living from touring the country. Shakespeare seems to have turned to poetry, producing the two long poems *Venus and Adonis* and *The Rape of Lucrece*, dedicated to his wealthy patron, the Earl of Southampton.

When the plague finally subsided in 1594, the theatres reopened and the acting companies regrouped as best they could. It was at this point that the Lord Chamberlain's Men were formed, with Shakespeare as one of their shareholders. It may not have been an easy decision for the young writer:

"At that time, he was torn between pursuing a career in the theatre and one in which he sought advancement by securing aristocratic patronage through his published poetry. For a while he had done both, but the rewards of patronage either didn't materialize or proved unsatisfying. Theatre won out ... After joining the Chamberlain's Men in 1594, Shakespeare hit his stride in the next two years with a great burst of innovative plays: A Midsummer Night's Dream, Love's Labour's Lost, Romeo and Juliet, King John, Richard the Second, The Merchant of Venice *and* The First Part of Henry the Fourth.*"*

James Shapiro, *1599: A Year in the Life of William Shakespeare*, 2005

Departures

Armado divides the participants into two groups, representing Spring, headed by the cuckoo, and Winter, led by the owl. Spring begins the song. It evokes the bright, fresh colours of the new season:

Spring: *When daisies pied[1] and violets blue,*
         And lady-smocks[2] all silver-white,
     And cuckoo-buds[3] of yellow hue
         Do paint the meadows with delight ...

     [1] *multicoloured*
     [2] *mayflowers*
     [3] *buttercups*

It is a time of activity, growth, and love, the song continues; the chorus, however, suggests that the word 'cuckoo', in its similarity to 'cuckold', might make married men uncomfortable. The cuckoo, moreover, is famed for laying its eggs in other birds' nests:

Spring: *The cuckoo then on every tree*
     Mocks married men, for thus sings he:
         'Cuckoo,
     Cuckoo, cuckoo!' O, word of fear,
     Unpleasing to a married ear!

Winter now responds, painting a picture of the harsh, unforgiving days of the year's end:

Winter: *When icicles hang by the wall,[1]*
         And Dick the shepherd blows his nail,[2]
     And Tom bears logs into the hall,
         And milk comes frozen home in pail,
     When blood is nipped and ways be foul[3] ...

     [1] *hang from the eaves*
     [2] *tries to warm his hands*
     [3] *when the blood is chilled, and the paths are muddy*

> *"One is set outside, the other inside; one is light, the other is dark. Yet spring is full of fear, winter of merriness ... it is hard not to feel that Shakespeare has deliberately defied and reversed expectations even in the play's last moments."*
>
> H. R. Woudhuysen, Introduction to the Arden Shakespeare edition of *Love's Labour's Lost*, 1998

This is a time when nature sleeps, a time of bitter weather and frail health. One sound, though, offers comfort to those huddled indoors as a warming meal is prepared:

Winter: *Then nightly sings the staring[1] owl:*
         'Tu-whit, Tu-whoo!'
   A merry note,
   While greasy Joan[2] doth keel[3] the pot.

   [1] *sharp-eyed*
   [2] *a poor, dirty woman*
   [3] *stir, tend to*

The song ends: and with that, Armado tells his audience, their pageant too comes to a close. Words can be jarring after the harmony of music, he accepts, so he will say no more. The performance is over. He ushers everyone away: the players of the Nine Worthies leave the stage to go back to their daily lives; the ladies depart for their year-long mourning in France; and the king and his lords return to the court of Navarre, their labour of love not yet won.

———
———

Acknowledgements

The following publications have proved invaluable as sources of factual information and critical insight:

- J. J. Anderson, *The Morality of* Love's Labour's Lost, Shakespeare Survey 24, Cambridge University Press, 1971

- Jonathan Bate, *Shakespeare's Career in the Theatre*, RSC Shakespeare edition of *Love's Labour's Lost*, Macmillan, 2008

- Jonathan Bate, *Soul of the Age*, Penguin, 2008

- Susan Baer Beck, Director's notes, Nebraska Shakespeare Festival, 1994

- Harold Bloom, *Shakespeare: The Invention of the Human*, HarperCollins, 1998

- Charles Boyce, *Shakespeare A to Z*, Roundtable Press, 1990

- Gavin Cameron-Webb, Director's notes, Colorado Shakespeare Festival, 2008

- William C. Carroll, Introduction to the New Cambridge Shakespeare edition of *Love's Labour's Lost*, Cambridge University Press, 2009

- Richard Dutton, *William Shakespeare: A Literary Life*, Macmillan, 1989

- Terry Eagleton, *William Shakespeare*, Blackwell, 1986

- Akiva Fox, *Trading Places*, Programme notes, Shakespeare Theatre Company, 2006

- D Scott Glasser, Director's notes, Nebraska Shakespeare Festival, 2007

- G. R. Hibbard, Introduction to the Oxford Shakespeare edition of *Love's Labour's Lost*, Oxford University Press, 1990

- Holly Kelsey, *Pestilence and Playwright*, Shakespeare Birthplace Trust, 2016

- James Shapiro, *1599: A Year in the Life of William Shakespeare*, Faber and Faber, 2005

- Greg Wells, *John Hall, Master of Physicke*, Manchester University Press, 2020

- Dr. Susan Willis, *Live and Learn: The Pursuit of Worthiness*, in *Asides*, Shakespeare Theatre Company, 2005

- H. R. Woudhuysen, Introduction to the Arden Shakespeare edition of *Love's Labour's Lost*, Bloomsbury, 1998

- Kevin Wright, *The Director's Cut*, RSC Shakespeare edition of *Love's Labour's Lost*, Macmillan, 2008

- Joanne Zipay, *Mistress Holofernes' Hornbook*, Programme notes, Judith Shakespeare Company, 2003

Guides currently available in the *Shakespeare Handbooks* series are:

- ❑ **Antony & Cleopatra** (ISBN 978 1 899747 02 3)
- ❑ **As You Like It** (ISBN 978 1 899747 00 9)
- ❑ **The Comedy of Errors** (ISBN 978 1 899747 16 0)
- ❑ **Coriolanus** (ISBN 978 1 899747 21 4)
- ❑ **Cymbeline** (ISBN 978 1 899747 20 7)
- ❑ **Hamlet** (ISBN 978 1 899747 07 8)
- ❑ **Henry IV, Part 1** (ISBN 978 1 899747 05 4)
- ❑ **Julius Caesar** (ISBN 978 1 899747 11 5)
- ❑ **King Lear** (ISBN 978 1 899747 03 0)
- ❑ **Love's Labour's Lost** (ISBN 978 1 899747 23 8)
- ❑ **Macbeth** (ISBN 978 1 899747 04 7)
- ❑ **Measure for Measure** (ISBN 978 1 899747 14 6)
- ❑ **The Merchant of Venice** (ISBN 978 1 899747 13 9)
- ❑ **The Merry Wives of Windsor** (ISBN 978 1 899747 18 4)
- ❑ **A Midsummer Night's Dream** (ISBN 978 1 899747 09 2)
- ❑ **Much Ado About Nothing** (ISBN 978 1 899747 17 7)
- ❑ **Othello** (ISBN 978 1 899747 12 2)
- ❑ **Richard II** (ISBN 978 1 899747 19 1)
- ❑ **Richard III** (ISBN 978 1 899747 22 1)
- ❑ **Romeo & Juliet** (ISBN 978 1 899747 10 8)
- ❑ **The Tempest** (ISBN 978 1 899747 08 5)
- ❑ **Twelfth Night** (ISBN 978 1 899747 01 6)
- ❑ **The Winter's Tale** (ISBN 978 1 899747 15 3)

www.shakespeare-handbooks.com